Learning from
No Child Left Behind

The Hoover Institution and Education Next Books gratefully acknowledge the following individuals and foundations for their support of this research on education policy and reform.

LYNDE AND HARRY BRADLEY FOUNDATION

KORET FOUNDATION

EDMUND AND JEANNIK LITTLEFIELD FOUNDATION

BERNARD AND CATHERINE SCHWARTZ FOUNDATION

WILLIAM E. SIMON FOUNDATION

BOYD AND JILL SMITH

TAD AND DIANNE TAUBE FOUNDATION

JACK AND MARY WHEATLEY

Learning from No Child Left Behind

How and Why the Nation's Most Important but Controversial Education Law Should Be Renewed

John E. Chubb

HOOVER INSTITUTION PRESS

STANFORD UNIVERSITY

STANFORD, CALIFORNIA

The Hoover Institution on War, Revolution and Peace, founded at Stanford University in 1919 by Herbert Hoover, who went on to become the thirty-first president of the United States, is an interdisciplinary research center for advanced study on domestic and international affairs. The views expressed in its publications are entirely those of the authors and do not necessarily reflect the views of the staff, officers, or Board of Overseers of the Hoover Institution.

www.hoover.org

An imprint of the Hoover Institution Press
Hoover Institution Press Publication No. 571

First printing, 2009
16 15 14 13 12 11 10 09   9 8 7 6 5 4 3 2 1

Manufactured in the United States of America

The paper used in this publication meets the minimum requirements of the American National Standard for Information Sciences— Permanence of Paper for Printed Library Materials, ANSI Z39.48–1992. ∞

Library of Congress Cataloging-in-Publication Data
Chubb, John E.
    Learning from No Child Left Behind : how and why the nation's most important but controversial education law should be renewed / by John E. Chubb.
        p.   cm.
    Includes bibliographical references and index.
    ISBN 978-0-8179-4982-2 (pbk. : alk. paper)
    1. United States. No Child Left Behind Act of 2001. 2. Educational accountability— Law and legislation—United States. 3. Education—Standards—United States. 4. Education—United States—Evaluation. 5. Educational equalization—United States. I. Title.
LB2806.22.C47 2009
379.1'580973—dc22   2009007008

Contents

Preface

No federal policy is as important to the future of education in America as No Child Left Behind (NCLB). Since its passage in 2002, the law has provided the nation with ambitious goals, concrete timetables, and potent remedies for raising student achievement and providing *every* American child a decent education. This is historic stuff, in a country that has long left education policy to the states and local school districts. With NCLB, the United States has committed itself to solving, as a nation, the education problems that have stymied policymakers since at least 1983, when a federal blue ribbon panel confirmed with *A Nation at Risk* the severity of the situation: achievement in math and science that lags many other nations around the world and gaps in achievement at home, between Blacks, Hispanics, and whites that leave most minority students ill prepared for life after high school.

But no federal education policy is as controversial as NCLB either. The law requires that students be tested in reading and math every year beginning at grade 3, and holds schools accountable for helping ever increasing portions of their students demonstrate proficiency every year. By 2014, the law requires that schools bring 100 percent of their students to proficiency. If schools fail to make sufficient progress, the law allows students to choose other schools and receive tutoring at district expense. Schools that fail to make adequate progress face increasing sanctions, including the possibility of closure. Public educators generally oppose the law, arguing that the expectations and sanctions are unfair and under-funded. State policymakers, sympathetic to the cries of educators, have shaped their own education laws, including especially their academic standards and definitions of proficiency, to make things easier for educators—thereby weakening NCLB. Critics of the law sometimes ridicule the very purpose of NCLB, to ensure that *every* child is proficient in the near future. But it should come as no surprise that a law that attempts to do as much as NCLB attempts to do, or that does so by upsetting the historical balance between federal and state power, should generate controversy. This is to be expected. Real change never comes easy.

As President Obama and Congress work to reverse the worst economic slide since the Great Depression, it is all the more important that the nation's education problems remain a top priority. Economic growth depends ever more strongly on the quality of education; the stronger a nation's education system, the greater the returns in the international marketplace. The president clearly appreciates this, and has won support for an $800 billion economic stimulus plan that promises to boost federal education spending in the short run and the long by tens of billions of dollars a year—doubling federal support for public schools. But this spending will be a missed opportunity if the money is not spent in ways that, while staving a financial crisis also promote fundamental school reform. NCLB can and will help guide this massive infusion of funds. But no one knows for how long. NCLB, which is authorized by Title I of the Elementary and Secondary Education Act, is operating under a temporary authorization, and needs to be reauthorized. Arne Duncan, the new secretary of education, indicates that

NCLB's reauthorization is in fact a top priority for the administration, but has not set a schedule for getting it done.

What should the administration do? In anticipation of the challenges facing the new administration, and the criticality of NCLB to education in the United States, the Hoover Institution Task Force on K–12 Education took up this question in 2008, giving the law as much time as possible to surface issues, self correct and otherwise prove its mettle. We had studied the law during its early days, and written in *Within Our Reach: How America Can Educate Every Child*, that NCLB had historic potential but significant weaknesses that we urged policymakers address. In the years since, the US Department of Education has ameliorated some of these issues. More important, the law has developed a track record that permits a more rigorous examination of its effects. Six years of test scores have piled up since NCLB became law. Researchers have begun more nuanced analyses. The Task Force reviewed the data and the extant research. We looked at the direct evidence of NCLB's consequences. We also considered the evidence, which is more abundant, on the principles on which NCLB rests: accountability, transparency, school choice, standards, teacher effectiveness, and much more. We debated, vigorously on most issues, and came to the conclusions we share here.

Several conclusions stand out. First, the nation *is* making academic progress. Student achievement is increasing, after a generation of stagnation, especially for the disadvantaged students that NCLB sought most directly to help. Second, as students are learning, we are learning more as a nation about what really works to raise student achievement. Third, while it would be premature to ascribe achievement gains directly to NCLB, it is safe to say that the principles on which NCLB is based provide an empirically sound foundation for serious school reform. Fourth, NCLB contains elements of unfairness, some of its provisions do not work nearly as well as they could, and at least one provision does not work at all. Finally, NCLB should be reauthorized, but with major defects corrected—as we outline with ten lessons to be learned and recommendations for improvement.

These ten points and the analysis that supports them constitute a coherent proposal for continuing the improvement of public education. The passage of NCLB did not start a reform process, nor should it be the end of one. NCLB was more a capstone event in a reform process that began twenty years earlier and that we strongly urge continue. NCLB was the culmination of a process that began with the national call to arms in *A Nation at Risk* and gained steam with the growing willingness of policymakers to adopt reforms that truly challenged the status quo. NCLB embraces these principles like no other law before it, and deserves support for this reason. Every member of the Task Force on K–12 Education supports these principles and, with one exception, endorsed the package of recommendations shared here. This does not mean that every Task Force member endorsed every element of every recommendation; they did not. But they supported the analysis and recommendations overall, reflecting confidence in both NCLB and in the larger process of fundamental reform of which NCLB is a part.

Supporters of the Task Force recommendations are a diverse and distinguished group of education scholars: economists Rick Hanushek and Caroline Hoxby of Stanford University; psychologist Herbert Walberg, emeritus professor from the University of Illinois; policy analysts Chester Finn, Jr., of the Fordham Foundation, Paul Hill of the University of Washington, Tom Loveless of the Brookings Institution; and political scientists Terry Moe of Stanford University, and Paul Peterson of Harvard and Stanford Universities. As author of the study I was responsible for leading the analysis and distilling our collective ideas into a coherent package that we could all support. I am a political scientist, a distinguished visiting scholar at the Hoover Institution, and an officer of EdisonLearning, a company that partners with public schools, typically serving disadvantaged students, to raise student achievement. Only one task force member chose not to endorse the overall report—though she supported various recommendations. That is Diane Ravitch, historian with New York University, whose views on NCLB are being published in *Education Next*. An additional Task Force member, Williamson Evers, was on leave from the Task Force during the project and did not participate in it.

Reform of an institution as venerable as public education is inevitably difficult. Disagreement and opposition are par for the course. Controversy comes with the territory. But public education is changing, and for the better. NCLB did not begin the change and will not end it. But NCLB is part of a longer process that is addressing the nation's lagging achievement at its core. The nation should take pride in the difficult decisions already made, learn from experience, correct clear mistakes, and continue down the path that NCLB has helped to blaze. The nation and our children will be smarter for it.

JOHN E. CHUBB
February 2009

Learning From
No Child Left Behind

Make no mistake: the United States has an education problem. American students trail students in many other nations in math and science achievement. Only one-third of American students achieve proficiency in reading and math by our nation's own standards. Two-thirds of African American and Hispanic students achieve well below grade level. Educational problems beget economic and social problems. The nation would be significantly richer, more competitive, and less divided were we better and more equitably educated.[1]

But the nation is also making progress. We are starting to learn. Students are making gains, slow and uneven to be sure but gains

---

1. The achievement percentages reference the *National Assessment of Education Progress* (U.S. Department of Education, Institute of Education Sciences, National Center for Education Statistics), the only nationally representative assessment of student achievement. As we shall discuss, state assessments report higher levels of achievement than NAEP but do so by setting lower performance expectations than NAEP does. We believe, with the support of international assessments such as Trends in International Math and Science Study (TIMSS) and the Program for International Assessment (PISA) in math, science, and reading, that the NAEP judgments are close to the mark. Our evaluation is supported by other education indicators such as four-year-high-school drop-out rates, which show less than 50 percent of students completing high school in many urban areas. Drop-out rates such as these are consistent with

nonetheless. More important, at least for now, we are starting to understand much better than ever before how to help students learn. Over the last generation, the nation has been ambitious about school reform. Yes, a lot of traditional measures have been applied— more money, smaller classes—but so too have bolder, innovative ideas such as academic standards backed by meaningful account-ability, report cards that make transparent school and potentially teacher performance, more opportunities for all families to choose their schools, and more competition for schools to satisfy students and parents. For these ideas, and many more, there is increasing evidence about what works, what does not, what is most important for student achievement, and what is less so.

A generation ago, achievement was worse than it is today, but worse still was our state of knowledge about how to improve mat-ters. *A Nation at Risk*, now twenty-five years old, is widely regarded as the modern call to arms for school improvement.[2] It docu-mented very ably just how dire the nation's achievement problem had become. American students performed in the middle of the pack internationally, domestic test scores—the SAT, the National Assessment of Education Progress (NAEP)—had been falling since the 1960s, and the country's economy had just been battered

NAEP estimates that two-thirds of black and Hispanic students, who predominate in urban areas, score "below basic," meaning far below grade level. See also, Organi-zation for Economic Cooperation and Development, Programme for International Assessment, *PISA 2006: Science Competencies for Tomorrow's World*; Organization for Economic Cooperation and Development, Programme for International Assessment, *Learning for Tomorrow's World: First Results from PISA 2003*; U.S. Department of Education, Institute of Education Sciences, National Center for Education Statistics, *Trends in International Math and Science Study* (2007).

2. U.S. Department of Education, National Commission on Excellence in Edu-cation, *A Nation at Risk: The Imperative for Educational Reform* (Washington, D.C., April 1983).

by a decade of international competition. The situation was grave, the report argued, a veritable national security risk. In retrospect, its recommendations seem mild, focusing mostly on beefing up high school curricula. In its wake, high school requirements were raised, students began taking more academic courses, and schools received much more funding. Yet by 1990 achievement had not improved materially.

An important lesson was slowly being learned, however. Achievement was not going to rise without more creative and stronger measures. Throughout the 1990s, the country made more fundamental changes. The public school system was opened to alternative approaches largely through charter schools. Regular public schools faced competition for students and resources, as a matter of public policy, for the first time in history. Likewise without precedent, policymakers began to set standards for what students should learn and held schools accountable for results. Most of this action was taken by the states, with encouragement from the bully pulpit in Washington.

In 2002 the federal government returned to the forefront—in potentially historic fashion. With the passage of No Child Left Behind (NCLB), supported by bipartisan majorities in Congress, the nation committed itself to the achievement of every student in America. The act set a concrete goal and deadline—universal proficiency in 2014. It backed its ambitions with a comprehensive system of accountability that was to touch every school in the country. For the United States, a federal system that has long reserved education for the states and school districts, NCLB was bold indeed.

However noble, firm measures often generate resistance. NCLB has faced controversy and criticism ever since it took effect. Educators largely do not like it. States chafe at the incursion on their historical turf. Because the law was vigorously advocated by President

George W. Bush, and implemented by his Department of Education, it has become something of a political lightning rod, easily attacked by opponents as a tool of a Republican president—and an unpopular one as well.

With the election of President Barack Obama, education will receive renewed attention in Washington. NCLB will inevitably be a focus. The law is due for reauthorization, operating now under a temporary extension, as Congress awaits guidance from a new administration. NCLB is the largest source of federal funds to school districts, itself a reauthorization of Title I of the Elementary and Secondary Education Act, channeling some $13 billion annually to schools with disadvantaged students. President Obama has expressed support for the law and clearly favors sending more federal dollars to needy schools.

President Obama also knows of the discontent with NCLB. The general pubic is losing faith in the law. A 2008 *Education Next/PEPG* survey found only 50 percent of the public favoring reauthorization, down from 57 percent in 2007.[3] The same poll found nearly half of all public school teachers wanting the law abolished. Teacher unions were the largest institutional contributors to the new president's election. NCLB reauthorization faces a strong political headwind.

Yet NCLB has strong forces behind it. The law was a culmination of decades of education policymaking in Congress. Education leaders there take a balanced view of the law's first eight years. They worked long and hard to put in place the law's basic principles. In exchange for federal dollars, they want meaningful accountability for student achievement. If schools fail to become places where

3. William G. Howell, Martin R. West, and Paul E. Peterson, "The 2008 Education Next-PEPG Survey of Public Opinion," *Education Next* (Fall 2008, vol. 8, no. 4), p. 16.

students can receive a decent education, they want students to have alternatives and schools to face real sanctions. They want schools to measure up to high academic standards and their performance to be transparent to families and communities. In the end, they recognize that bold and innovative policies are bound to get some things wrong and require adjustment. NCLB is sound in its fundamentals, they believe, but its particulars need serious attention.

This viewpoint, we believe, is correct. Despite the controversy that NCLB has ignited, the law is making a positive difference. Students are learning. Policymakers are learning. Because of NCLB and the state laws that served as its precedent, our collective knowledge of how to make schools work has grown substantially. NCLB deserves to be reauthorized. It also needs to be improved. It contains elements of unfairness; several parts do not work well and require significant modification. At least one major piece should be scrapped altogether and replaced. The law requires more than minor fine-tuning, yet it also deserves credit and support. As we shall share, it has helped students achieve, and it has taught us how to drive educational improvement more successfully.

Student Achievement

Eight years into the NCLB era, the United States is still very much at risk educationally. There must be no confusion about this point. Evidence comes from multiple sources, beginning with our own National Assessment of Education Progress, most recently administered in 2007. In the foundation subjects of reading and math, our levels of achievement are unacceptably low.[4] Looking across the three tested grade levels—fourth, eighth, and twelfth—only *one-third*

---

4. NAEP is not a perfect measure of achievement—nothing is. Some mathematicians argue that NAEP assessments in grade eight contain too much lower level mathematics, particularly whole number sense, and not enough fractions, decimals, and pre-algebra. NAEP math also places a premium on the ability to solve word problems, a product of the frameworks from the National Council of Teachers of Mathematics on which NAEP is based. Because NAEP has arguably insufficient higher level math content, students must score very well to be declared proficient. The test may therefore understate math proficiency. However, an international exam that mathematicians regard as more rigorous, TIMSS, shows middling levels of math achievement as well, particularly if the test's limited country sample is kept in mind. An international comparison of math achievement including all OECD countries and samples of 15-year-olds, PISA, finds US students in the bottom quartile in math achievement. On the weaknesses of NAEP math assessments, see Tom Loveless, "Is Proficiency on NAEP Set Too High?" *Brown Center Report on American Education* (Washington, D.C.: Brookings Institution, 2007), pp. 10–13. NAEP's assessment of reading skills is more widely accepted as accurate. NAEP, we should also recognize, is the product of the work of highly regarded psychometricians and

of all students on average are "proficient" or "advanced" in reading. In math, the average proficient or advanced rate is also about one-third, though it declines markedly with age, from about 40 percent at grade four to less than 25 percent in grade twelve. What this means, in practical terms, is that only a third of American young people are demonstrating full mastery of the knowledge and skills that education experts believe appropriate for their respective grade levels. For perspective, in the highest achieving nations in the world, two-thirds of all students demonstrate proficiency by NAEP standards.[5]

For American students falling short of proficiency, the picture is even grimmer. Like most tests that measure students against objective standards (rather than against other students), NAEP establishes categories of performance to reflect distinct levels of mastery. If students do not reach full mastery—or proficiency—they can be considered "basic" if they show understanding of certain essentials of a subject or "below basic" if they fall short of grasping even the essentials. Falling below basic generally means performing several grade levels below age expectations. Based on the latest NAEP, roughly *one-third* of all students are achieving below basic. At this level, students leave high

---

education content specialists, overseen by a bipartisan panel of national experts, the National Assessment Governing Board. The NAEP scores reported in this section are from the main NAEP, 2006 for reading and 2007 for math. See also, Organization for Economic Cooperation and Development, Programme for International Assessment, *PISA 2006: Science Competencies for Tomorrow's World*; Organization for Economic Cooperation and Development, Programme for International Assessment, *Learning for Tomorrow's World: First Results from PISA 2003*; U.S. Department of Education, Institute of Education Sciences, National Center for Education Statistics, *Trends in International Math and Science Study* (2007).

5. For estimates of how other nations might perform on NAEP, see Gary W. Phillips, "Linking NAEP Achievement Levels to TIMSS" (Washington, D.C.: American Institutes for Research, April 2007).

school utterly unprepared for college or demanding work—if they graduate from high school at all. For the nation's black and Hispanic students, these numbers are worse still. *Two-thirds* on average score below basic in reading and in math.[6] It is no surprise that urban dropout rates now frequently exceed 50 percent.[7]

No Child Left Behind focuses on reading and math—so the law has certainly not cured what ails us. Yet, in fields that NCLB has hardly touched, science and history, matters are even more troubling. Science achievement is critical to many of the economic opportunities of the future. History is vital to citizenship at home and in the larger world that is ever more relevant to our young people. By NAEP standards, achievement in these areas is abysmal. About 15 percent of American students, again averaging across fourth, eighth, and twelfth grades, are proficient or advanced in history. In science the average is less than 25 percent.[8]

The national data are reinforced by international data. Questions are sometimes raised whether NAEP performance levels are set too high, providing an unnecessarily discouraging view of US achievement.[9] Fewer students score as proficient on NAEP than

6. Concomitantly, few black and Hispanic students score proficient or advanced. Less than 15 percent of black students, averaged across fourth, eighth, and twelfth grade, reach these levels in reading. Only 10 percent meet these standards in math. The patterns are the same for Hispanic students, but with average scores about 3 percentage points higher. These data and other averages cited in the text have been collected from the NAEP Data Explorer data tool on the NAEP web site. Go to http://nces.ed.gov/nationsreportcard/naepdata/.

7. Jay P. Greene and Marcus A. Winters, "Leaving Boys Behind: Public High School Graduation Rates," Civic Report No. 48 (New York: Manhattan Institute, April 2006).

8. Go to http://nces.ed.gov/nationsreportcard/naepdata/.

9. When NAEP is equated to international tests such as TIMSS, high achieving nations such as Singapore, outperform the United States by more than 2 to 1.

on any state achievement test. But when US students are compared to students internationally, the picture of underachievement remains the same. The most comprehensive international measure is the Program for International Assessment (PISA), which compares thirty Organization for Economic Cooperation and Development (OECD) nations.[10] The last two assessments, in 2003 and 2006, found US 15-year-olds, the age group tested, below the middle of the pack in math and science. The 2006 study showed US students in twenty-first place out of thirty nations in science and twenty-fifth out of thirty in math. What NAEP indicates about math and science achievement—that US students generally score low—is reinforced by comparisons with many other nations.

Weak achievement in school translates into weak achievement after graduation. Although the United States has a university system that is the envy of the world—and enrolls large numbers of international students—Americans do not take full advantage. Only 30 percent of American young people earn bachelor's degrees, a middling percentage relative to other nations. In 1995, the United States led the world in college degrees; today we are not in the top

---

In eighth grade math, 73 percent of all Singapore students would score proficient or better on NAEP. The proficiency standard set by NAEP is clearly achievable by the vast majority of students in a high-achieving nation. This begs the question as to whether NAEP is too high a standard to benchmark NCLB, which has a 100 percent proficiency goal. But even if NAEP is too high of a standard to insist every student in the nation meet it, it is clearly not a standard that is too high for understanding whether American students are satisfying reasonably high expectations. For a critical discussion of this point, see Loveless, "Is Proficiency on NAEP Set Too High?"

10. Organization for Economic Cooperation and Development, Programme for International Assessment, *PISA 2006: Science Competencies for Tomorrow's World*; Organization for Economic Cooperation and Development, Programme for International Assessment, *Learning for Tomorrow's World: First Results from PISA 2003*.

ten.[11] Few Americans secure advanced degrees in technical fields—
what the twenty-first century demands. For example, in 2005,
among master's and doctoral degrees earned by US students, 13.7
percent were in science and 6.4 percent in engineering. Among Japanese students, 38.5 percent were in science and the same percentage in engineering.[12]

These test scores matter, not only for the welfare of individual students but for the welfare of the nation as whole. Extensive
research shows that individuals who obtain higher test scores on
standardized achievement tests do better in the labor market. Similarly, the distribution of skills measured by achievement tests affects
the distribution of income in society: chronic underperformance
by low-income and minority students generates income disparities
later in life. Finally, standardized test scores predict the acquisition of skills that affect the growth of national income and thus the
future well-being of society.[13]

This is an alarming and frustratingly familiar story. Policymakers have been hearing it since A Nation at Risk. The US has been
behind other nations at least that long. NAEP scores have shown
low levels of proficiency and gaping racial differences in achievement

11. On higher education performance and other pertinent international comparisons, see National Governors Association, Council of Chief State School Officers, and Achieve, Inc., Benchmarking for Success: Ensuring U.S. Students Receive a
World-Class Education (Washington, D.C.: December 2008).

12. U.S. Department of Education, Institute of Education Sciences, National
Center for Education Statistics, Digest of Education Statistics (2005).

13. See Eric A. Hanushek and Ludger Woessmann, "The Role of Cognitive
Skills in Economic Development," Journal of Economic Literature (Summer 2008,
vol. 43, no. 3), pp. 607–668; Eric A. Hanushek, "Some Simple Analytics of School
Quality," NBER Working Paper (no. 10229, January 2004); Eric Hanushek, Dean
T. Jamison, Eliot A. Jamison, and Ludger Woessmann, "Education and Economic
Growth," Education Next (Summer 2008, vol. 8, no. 2), pp. 62–70.

since then as well. But amidst these persistent causes for concern are genuine reasons for hope. Levels of achievement are low to be sure, but the nation's students have been making progress, and the progress is increasingly well understood.

Let us reexamine NAEP. In the 1990s, before NCLB and before most states implemented accountability systems, US fourth graders scored 12 percent proficient or above in math—just 12 percent. Since 2000, the average has risen to 39 percent, a threefold increase. Among white fourth graders, proficient or advanced scores jumped from 15 to 51 percent, among blacks from 1 to 15 percent, and among Hispanics from 4 to 22 percent. At grade eight, the gains in math were not quite as large, but dramatic nonetheless: 15 to 31 percent overall, 18 to 41 percent among whites, 5 to 11 percent among blacks, and 7 to 15 percent among Hispanics. By any standard these are very large gains.[14]

In reading, progress has also occurred. It has been slower, as reading gains typically are. Reading is a skill heavily influenced by the home and community environment and harder for schools to drive than is math. Yet, in grades four and eight, overall scores of proficient or advanced rose 5 percent from the 1990s to the 2000s. Among white students the gains averaged 7 points, among black students 5 points, and among Hispanic students 4 points.

These gains are consistent with the implementation of NCLB and the state accountability systems that set the precedent for

14. The gains on NAEP math are greater than on international measures of math achievement. The NAEP measures are based on the standards of the National Council of Teachers of Mathematics (NCTM) and emphasized problem-solving skills over more traditional skills of number sense. The NAEP math standards are also arguably lower than international standards. Nonetheless, US students made great strides on the NAEP math assessment, likely reflecting genuine learning of the NCTM-based curriculum being taught in the country from the late 1980s forward. On the issues with NAEP math standards and assessments, see Loveless, "Is Proficiency on NAEP Set Too High?"

NCLB. It is far too early to estimate with confidence the impact that NCLB has had on rising math and reading scores. But more disaggregated views of NAEP data point to NCLB as a possible cause. A recent study by the Thomas B. Fordham Institute examined the achievement of two important subgroups—the lowest achieving 10 percent of the population, or the students most at risk of being "left behind," and the top 10 percent of the distribution, or the students some fear NCLB may cause to be neglected. That analysis found very impressive gains by the lowest 10 percent in math from 2000 to 2007: 18 scale points at grade four and 13 scale points at grade eight. Roughly 11 scale points represent one grade equivalent. In the brief NCLB era, then, the nation's lowest students gained materially in math. Happily, math gains were also made by the top students, though not as great as the lowest students: 10 and 5 scale points in grades four and eight respectively.[15]

In reading, the news was very good at grade four for the lowest 10 percent: skills rose 16 points on the NAEP scale. Again, this gain was from just 2000 to 2007. Top students improved, but only by 3 points over this time span. In grade eight reading, the pattern was not so encouraging: the lowest students gained zero while the top students lost 3 points. Nevertheless, in math large gains were made by both subgroups at both grades. In grade four reading the weakest students progressed more than a grade equivalent while top students inched forward. In both subjects and grade levels, the gap in achievement between top and bottom narrowed.

15. Ann Duffett, Steve Farkas, and Tom Loveless, *High Achieving Students in the Era of No Child Left Behind* (Washington, D.C.: Thomas B. Fordham Institute, June 2008). Note that the scale scores used to describe NAEP achievement in this study are different from the proficiency levels used earlier in our analysis. The scale scores underlie the proficiency levels and allow finer measurement of student progress than do the proficiency levels, each of which subsumes a range of scale points.

The Fordham study also examined whether the gains that occurred after 2000 were unique to this NCLB era or were continuations of trends that began in the 1990s. The lowest NAEP achievement decile gained at a significantly higher rate during the NCLB era than during the 1990s. The highest achievement decile gained at about the same rate in both eras. Overall, it appears that reforms during the 1990s, largely at the state levels, promoted achievement gains in reading and especially in math. During the 2000s, these gains continued but accelerated for the lowest achieving students.[16]

Progress in reading and math, however, has not been replicated in science and history. Scores from the 1990s and 2000s are virtually identical—and low. This is obviously not part of the good-news story, but it is relevant to the tale of progress. The NCLB era that began as the legislation took shape in 2001, and the accountability era that began in the states in the 1990s, have been associated with substantial achievement gains in math and lesser gains in reading—without question. The focus of these times has been sharply on

16. To be clear, the Fordham study could not associate the gains after 2000 with NCLB directly. Implementation of NCLB did not begin until 2002, and some of the post-2000 gains occurred in 2001. Temporally, most of the post-2000 gains did occur after NCLB took effect, *suggesting* cause and effect. A federal analysis of Title I found much the same patterns as the Fordham study. The Institute of Education Sciences conducted a comprehensive assessment of Title I, as required by NCLB. Its October 2007 final report found that students in high-poverty schools were making larger gains on NAEP in reading and math than students in low-poverty schools, since both 2000 and 2003, when NCLB took effect. U.S. Department of Education, Institute of Education Sciences, National Center for Education Evaluation and Regional Assistance, *National Assessment of Title I: Final Report*, vol. 1, *Implementation* (Washington, DC, October 2007), pp. 38–43. Still, more research will be needed to determine how much NCLB and other factors contributed to the post-2000 gains in reading and math.

improving math and reading skills. Science and social studies have been of secondary concern in the states, if considered at all. The lack of progress in these subjects is consistent with the hypothesis that NCLB and state accountability requirements are having an impact. As we shall see subsequently, there is additional evidence that accountability is working.[17]

Policymakers must continue to approach the nation's education problems with urgency. Achievement remains low and its gaps remain wide. But policymakers should also pay close attention to the progress that has been made. Gains in test scores and reductions in achievement gaps are likely no accident. They parallel bold policies that began to be put in place by the states and culminated with the federal government's enactment of NCLB. There are lessons now to be learned. We should acknowledge our progress and build thoughtfully upon it.

17. Go to http://nces.ed.gov/nationsreportcard/naepdata/.

Lessons and Recommendations

1. Academic standards are critical to raising student achievement, but the disparities among state standards and the weakness of many state standards, unfortunately encouraged by NCLB, are simply bad for students. NCLB should be amended to promote the development and implementation of a voluntary system of *national academic standards*.

No Child Left Behind, as we have said, is a potentially historic act. Through NCLB the nation made what amounts to a moral commitment to the education of every American child. In the future, every student will be educated to a level of "proficiency" in reading and in math. The United States once led the world in democratizing schooling, being among the first to guarantee every child a free public education. NCLB goes a major step further, promising not only to provide education but to ensure that education works. This is unprecedented; no other nation on the planet has committed itself to universal achievement—an auspicious democratic ideal indeed.

But NCLB had to make its commitment for not only a nation, but for a nation of states. Education is not a federal responsibility in the United States; the Constitution leaves it to the states. And historically, the states have discharged the responsibility by delegating it to local school districts. Today, the states and districts provide nearly 95 percent of school funding—about 50 percent of which is provided by each of these entities—and the federal government uses its share of funds to protect civil rights and support the needs of underserved groups such as economically disadvantaged students, English language learners, and students with special needs. NCLB sought to leverage the federal government's support for economically disadvantaged students to create a national system of standards and accountability that would apply to all students, regardless of economic need. But it had to do so with the support of fifty states with disparate educational expectations and the long-standing prerogative to run their own education systems.

The result is the now notorious NCLB compromise which allowed each state to set its own academic standards and to provide its own definition of proficiency—notorious, because after eight years of NCLB, the compromise has so obviously failed to do what Congress and the president hoped it would do. Proficiency was intended in the law to provide students with the knowledge and skills to work effectively at each grade level from elementary school through high school. Proficiency was meant to prepare students to leave high school well prepared for the next step, whatever it might be. The law assumed the states would all want proficiency to accomplish the same things. But the states have not interpreted the law that way.

Very few states have established what experts agree are strong standards. To help students and schools excel—to educate for the demands of the twenty-first century—standards need to be clear and rigorous about the content as well as the skills that must be mastered. The standards should be derived from expectations about what students ultimately need when they leave high school—the ability to enter college or a demanding postsecondary training program and to succeed without remediation. Unfortunately, most state standards fall short of satisfying all or even many of these criteria. Standards are often overly general about the nature of requisite skills, open-ended about content, and vague about levels of mastery. The Thomas B. Fordham Foundation awards only three states—California, Indiana, and Massachusetts—A grades for their reading, mathematics, science, and history standards taken as whole.[18] Only six states earn Bs; most earn low grades, with 21 Ds and three Fs. States have seldom written standards that match what students require for college or careers. Achieve, Inc., a highly respected national bipartisan organization launched by governors and business leaders, estimates that no more than three states have high school standards and accountability systems fully aligned with college and careers.[19]

Compounding the difficulty, states have been generally undemanding of student performance. Even if standards provide decent guidance regarding what should be taught and learned, states have been willing to declare students "proficient" without them scoring at high levels on their respective assessments. As with standards, a few states have set their bar—or proficiency score—high: South Carolina, Massachusetts, Missouri, and Hawaii have proficiency "cut points" at grades four and eight that yield estimates of student

18. Chester E. Finn, Jr., Liam Julian, and Michael Petrilli, 2006 *The State of State Standards* (Washington, D.C.: Thomas B. Fordham Foundation, August 2006). Note that organizations of every political persuasion agree that state standards leave much to be desired. See, for example, the standards evaluations of the American Federation of Teachers.

19. *2008 Closing the Expectations Gap* (Washington, D.C.: Achieve, Inc., February 2008).

proficiency similar to what NAEP estimates for their states. We say "high" because NAEP rates fewer students proficient in every state than the states themselves do, meaning that NAEP has the highest proficiency bar in the nation.[20]

NCLB also requires that state proficiency scores be compared to, or "benchmarked" against, NAEP. This is valuable, for regardless of whether NAEP is on the mark for what America's standards and proficiency levels ought to be, it provides a common metric against which each state can be judged. Unfortunately, the metric finds the states all over the map with performance levels—and generally well below NAEP. On average, states claim proficiency percentages, gauged by their own tests, which are two to four times the levels measured by NAEP. In fourth grade math, for example, the average difference between NAEP-measured and state-measured state proficiency levels is thirty-two percentage points. The states with the lowest proficiency thresholds—Tennessee, Oklahoma, Georgia, Nebraska, West Virginia, Mississippi, and Alabama—rate their students fifty to sixty percentage points more proficient than NAEP rates them.

There is no reason why students in different American states should face such disparate expectations in school. No one would argue that students in Mississippi should be held to lower standards in reading and math than students in, say, Massachusetts—as if these basic subjects are not as important in some states as in others. Yet that is current reality. Even neighboring states have vastly different standards. North Carolina claims nearly 50 percent more

20. We want to emphasize that standards must provide sound content guidance as well as demanding performance levels. It is hardly a virtue if a state provides poor content standards but high proficiency bars or vice versa. What good does it do to score well on a bad test or be held to low expectations on a good one? States are guilty of both.

proficient students in reading and math than does South Carolina, even though NAEP says the two states achieve at similar levels. The average student declared proficient on the North Carolina exam would not be proficient on the South Carolina exam.

NCLB has not helped matters. Before NCLB, states set academic standards and also set the consequences attached to them. A state could decide to set expectations high and then build an accountability system it considered fair—giving schools adequate time and resources to meet the standards. Since NCLB, states have had to consider not only the consequences they may attach to standards but the consequences NCLB attaches to them as well. Many states have decided that the consequences of NCLB are too onerous and have moved to shield their schools from them—by lowering standards, making it easier for students to be proficient and schools to make adequate yearly progress (AYP). A recent study of 2007 NAEP and state test scores shows that state proficiency standards have declined since NCLB and begun a slow process of convergence—to a lower average level.[21] The pattern is not perfect; some states have raised their proficiency thresholds from low levels to moderate levels. And the process is rather slow; there is no evidence that states are racing to drop their standards to whatever level, no matter how low, necessary to declare every child proficient in 2014.[22] But it is clear that, motivated in part by the NCLB requirements that every student be "proficient," many states have decided that skills that NAEP calls "basic" are good enough to be "NCLB

21. Paul E. Peterson and Frederick M. Hess, "Few States Set World-Class Standards," *Education Next* (Summer 2008, vol. 8, no. 3), pp. 70–73.

22. The lack of an outright "race to the bottom" for state proficiency levels is demonstrated by Tom Loveless, "Are States Honestly Reporting Test Scores?" *The Brown Center Report on American Education* (Washington, D.C.: Brookings Institution, 2006), pp. 22–30.

proficient." This is sad, because the moral expectation of NCLB was that when students were proficient, it would mean something worthwhile.

Unless state standards and proficiency thresholds change, the nation will continually deceive itself—and the students and families who live in states with low expectations—that education progress is being made. It is time for the deception to end. The nation needs national standards if it is to make good on the commitment that NCLB expressed sincerely on behalf of a bipartisan and overwhelming majority of Congress—and the American people. Lawmakers shied from national standards when NCLB was drafted in 2001, remembering the bitter disputes among states and interest groups that attended efforts during the Clinton administration to write national standards. But eight years has changed perspectives. State standards are widely recognized as a problem, and informal efforts have begun to build consensus around what national standards might look like.

The Education Trust, a highly respected national advocacy organization for the educationally disadvantaged, has argued for "college and career ready" standards that could be written by a nonpartisan national panel. Achieve, Inc., supported by governors, business leaders, and the Gates Foundation, has enlisted thirty-four states, enrolling 85 percent of the nation's public school students, in the American Diploma Project, a voluntary effort to develop high school graduation requirements that truly prepare students for college and work. A similar consortium led by the National Governors Association recently tackled the controversial issue of how to measure high school drop-out rates. It recommended the forthright metric of four-year graduation or continued matriculation rates for all ninth graders. Even though the definition exposed drop-out rates in excess of 50 percent in numerous cities—over double the rates previously reported—the consortium was able to muster support for tightening the definition of dropouts. In 2008 the federal government embraced the definition for NCLB accountability. Most recently, the National Governors Association, the Council of Chief State School Officers, and Achieve, Inc. proposed a project to develop national academic standards explicitly benchmarked to international standards.[23] Finally, we must acknowledge that the country has long had a de facto national curriculum—the content of the few major textbooks used nationwide. It is time the nation set its curriculum directly and stopped deferring to commercial publishers.

We propose that NCLB be reauthorized with two new provisions. The first would be an explicit statement of what state standards in reading and math are required to accomplish. We propose that state standards be required to specify the knowledge and skills that *all* students are expected to attain in order to attend college or enter a promising career without remediation. The nation should embrace the explicit idea—espoused as an aspiration by NCLB—that public education is preparing students for a workplace in which a middle-class living standard requires education to a level of college readiness or its career equivalent. States should write high school reading and math standards that, if satisfied, will ensure every high school graduate a chance of academic and career success immediately thereafter. A high school diploma would, of course, depend on passing these tests: students must be accountable for their achievement along with everyone else. States should then write standards for grades K-8 that build toward these high school exit standards.

---

23. National Governors Association, Council of Chief State School Officers, and Achieve, Inc., *Benchmarking for Success: Ensuring U.S. Students Receive a World-Class Education* (Washington, D.C.: NGA, December 2008).

To be clear, these are standards for every student, excepting those with diagnosed impediments to satisfying them. They are standards to be set based on the empirical principle of readiness, in reading and math only, for success in college or a promising career. These are high standards given where the nation stands today, but they are not impractically high. They do not define a "world-class" education for every student or a rich liberal arts education for every student. These standards are meant to define the common core of foundation skills that are demonstrably necessary for success after high school in the twenty-first century. NCLB should be amended to be clear about these "core" standards—as we suggest they be called.

Second, NCLB should initiate and fund a process for writing core national standards and the tests to measure them. We propose that the Department of Education seek proposals for multistate consortia to develop core standards and tests, based on the principles of college and career readiness. Any consortium including at least five states would be eligible to apply. The Department would select and fund up to three consortia. Selections would need to be complete within one year of reauthorization. Standards and tests would need to be in place within two years. The new tests would need to satisfy several ongoing technical requirements. Tests would need to be based on sizable item banks that would permit all used test items to be released to the public after each test administration. Public knowledge builds public trust and also helps teachers prepare students to satisfy worthwhile standards. Tests would also need to be validated against post-high-school outcomes. NCLB would fund third-party evaluations of the relationship between high school test scores and subsequent student success in college and the labor market. The core standards must predict college and career readiness, as intended. Finally, test scores at grades twelve, eight, and four would be benchmarked against NAEP. It is vital that the core standards be calibrated against one common metric, and NAEP is the best metric available.

After reauthorization, states would have the option of joining any one of the three approved consortia and implementing their respective standards and measures. States would also have the option of going it on their own—but the incentives against doing so would be steep. States going it alone would still have to rewrite standards and tests to satisfy the new core requirements of college and career readiness. They would have to have third party validation of predictable college and labor market outcomes. They would have to maintain sizable item banks and release used items. They would have to do all of this at their expense. These are powerful disincentives.

Now, three sets of national standards may defy the term "national." But three is far fewer than fifty. More important, there is virtue in pursuing national standards through the principles of federalism. Allowing the states to coalesce behind several different approaches should yield fewer compromises of core principles than forcing a single national solution immediately. Allowing several consortia also reduces the chances that any one group or interest will dominate or control the process. States are already showing a willingness to seek credible national standards voluntarily, as they are doing via the National Diploma Project. NCLB will be facilitating a process that has already begun.

The big question, of course, is will greater clarity about the purpose of core standards, coupled with the requirements of demonstrable validity and full transparency, raise the nation's performance? Will more students measure up against NAEP proficiency standards or international ones? There are no guarantees. Strong standards and high proficiency bars do not ensure achievement; other factors, as we shall see, also drive achievement. Indeed, some states with excellent standards still lag in performance. But it is difficult to imagine achievement without explicit expectations for it. NCLB can do much to promote higher standards and to discourage their watering down. NCLB should do this by offering states the incentive to work with like-minded states to set standards that are meaningful for all of today's students and for which states want to be accountable.

2. NCLB laudably asks that "no child" go uneducated. Yet the law gives schools no credit in adequate yearly progress (AYP) calculations for students that make academic progress below and above a state's proficiency threshold, thereby discouraging schools from paying equal attention to the education of all students. NCLB should be amended to give schools AYP credit for *academic growth* **everywhere along the performance continuum, bottom to top, as long as it projects to proficiency by the end of high school. Schools should also receive** *financial rewards* **for students they help achieve at the highest levels. Finally, states should be provided incentive grants to develop online** *adaptive tests* **to provide the most reliable tests possible for students well below grade level and well above.**

Perhaps no provision of NCLB has generated more complaints from educators than the failure of the act to credit schools for the progress of students until they cross the proficiency hurdle. Especially for schools with large numbers of students progressing from below basic to basic—gains that are essential to get eventually to proficiency—this provision seems patently unfair. Unfairness generates frustration and even cynicism—manifested in the idea that the act is some sort of partisan conspiracy to punish low achieving schools—and this only makes it more difficult for NCLB to succeed.

The US Department of Education has recognized this flaw in the act and begun approving the use of "growth models" to measure AYP. As of January 2009, fifteen states had received approval, through reviews by a panel of widely respected technical experts and practitioners, to measure the growth of students toward proficiency—instead of merely counting students as they clear the proficiency bar. The growth models have had to satisfy so-called "bright line principles of NCLB," most importantly that all students will reach proficiency by 2014.[24] The growth models seek a fairer way of tracking student progress to NCLB's statutory goals.

The current growth models are a big step in the right direction, but they do not go far enough. NCLB runs the risk, even with growth models, of minimizing the needs of students once they reach proficiency. Under NCLB, schools receive no credit for helping students grow from proficient to advanced levels of achievement. With growth models, the same is true; maintaining proficient status year after year is all that matters. While NCLB's purpose was explicitly to ensure that all students achieve *at least* proficiency, and the law had no stated objectives for advanced students, the law never envisioned unintended consequences that might hurt top students. That prospect, however, is real. As we saw, the United States has reason to be concerned about the performance of its students at higher levels of achievement. Whether it is measured via test scores, bachelor's degrees, or advanced technical degrees, the top quartile of American students is not leading the world. We now know that since NCLB was adopted, top students are progressing at lower rates than students at the bottom.[25]

24. See "U.S. Secretary of Education Margaret Spellings Approves Additional Growth Model Pilots for 2007–2008 School Year," U.S. Department of Education, June 10, 2008.

25. Duffett, Farkas, and Loveless, *High Achieving Students in the Era of No Child Left Behind*.

Effects notwithstanding, NCLB offers schools no incentive to boost achievement beyond proficiency. This is even more concerning in the many states that have low standards for proficiency. It is also unnecessary. NCLB should be amended to define AYP as growth toward proficiency *and beyond*. Research on growth models has made very clear the trajectories that achievement can reasonably be expected to follow for students scoring at different achievement levels. Students who score below basic have trajectories that predict that most will remain below basic throughout their school careers. Only students learning at very high rates—say the ninetieth percentile of all below basic students—will eventually reach proficiency. The challenge varies with the rigor of state standards, but NCLB insists nonetheless that students overcome their historic trajectories and grow at whatever rate is necessary to reach proficiency. This is bold and good policy.

NCLB has very different expectations, however, for students who already score proficient or advanced. A proficient student likely need grow no more than the average for all proficient students to remain proficient. An advanced student faces even lower expectations. That student need not remain advanced to satisfy NCLB; proficient is good enough. An advanced student might need grow no more than the twentieth or thirtieth percentile of all advanced students to remain on a course for mere proficiency. This is clearly bad policy—an unintended consequence that makes no sense. NCLB should be asking schools to help *all* students *grow*—not just maintain, and certainly to not accept backsliding; yet NCLB does just that for proficient and advanced students.

NCLB should be amended to require growth models to measure AYP. The definition of AYP should then be changed as follows: all students, whether above or below proficiency, must make annual achievement gains sufficient to place them on a trajectory to score proficient by the time of their high school exit exam—but no later than grade eleven. For students scoring below proficiency, the trajectory will be steep, and ever more so the less time remains until the high school exit exam. But schools will appropriately get credit toward AYP for getting kids on a promising path, even if it will be several years until the student reaches proficiency. This policy change is eminently sensible and a huge improvement in fairness.

For students achieving above proficiency, the trajectory requirement is a reasonable safeguard against backsliding. Students who are losing ground will not count toward AYP if their decline projects out to a score below proficiency in eleventh grade. Schools may protest that students still scoring proficient ought to count toward AYP. But it is clearly better to catch achievement problems early, when interventions have maximum time to succeed, than to wait until a student has fallen from proficiency to call a school on the issue.

Yet schools and the nation deserve more from NCLB than a disincentive for higher achieving kids to fall backwards. We ought to be rewarding schools for helping students move beyond mere proficiency. Thus, we propose that NCLB be further modified to provide schools *financial rewards* for every student scoring proficient or above who is also on a trajectory to score *advanced* by the end of high school. We propose incentive grants of meaningful size—perhaps $150 per student per year, or about 25 percent of the typical per pupil Title I grant today. NCLB includes numerous sanctions, appropriate in our view. But good policy should have rewards as well as remedies—encouragement to go above and beyond and not just achieve the basics. America needs more students achieving at the highest levels, and NCLB ought to reward schools that produce them.

Schools must be credited with helping *all* students grow academically, and this proposal does just that. Every student is expected to be on track toward proficiency by high school graduation. Students who are on track count toward making AYP; students who are not on track, regardless of their current status, do not count. We want to emphasize that this proposal in no way allows the progress of high achievers to compensate for any lack of progress among low achievers; progress by high achievers yields incentive grants but no extra credit toward AYP. Unlike the current AYP system, schools have the potential to be credited for the progress of all of their students—the ones well below the proficiency bar but making good progress and the ones above the bar not resting on their laurels. Our proposal fixes the inequity in the current system for low and high achievers alike. Finally, our proposal leaves in tact the expectations that specific subgroups make AYP in addition to the school as a whole: no student is overlooked or undervalued.

Finally, a technical point: if we are going to serve the interests of all students from the highest achieving to the lowest, we must have reliable measures of their achievement. State-criterion-referenced tests are not designed to measure very well the achievement of students far from the middle of the achievement distribution. Tests have limited numbers of items, and few items are designed to gauge exactly what the top students or the students at the bottom know and can do. This can be remedied with "adaptive tests," delivered by computers, to ask students more questions at their own level of achievement and fewer questions that are too hard or too easy. The tests still measure where students are relative to their grade level standards but provide far better information about precisely what they need in order to achieve more. Teachers and students would benefit greatly from this superior information—and measurement would be more reliable and fairer too. NCLB should provide *incentive grants* to states to develop adaptive tests for approval by the

Department of Education and replacement of today's one-size-fits-all paper and pencil exams. Thousands of school districts already use commercially available adaptive tests for formative assessment purposes.[26] They can be designed for summative accountability as well. Adaptive testing is smarter, fairer—and feasible.

3. The evidence is becoming decisive: accountability works. But NCLB's accountability could work better. Effective accountability reinforces performance standards with appropriate incentives and sanctions. NCLB's accountability is too blunt an instrument. It imposes the same regimen of escalating annual incentives and sanctions on a wide range of school performances. Schools that fail to make AYP due to the performance of one subgroup should not be treated the same as schools that fail most of their students. NCLB should be amended to provide a *simple and differentiated system of incentives and sanctions*. The US Department of Education should be further empowered to support the system by maintaining on its website a user-friendly *national database* of the accountability status of every school in the nation.

NCLB did not begin the practice of holding schools accountable for student achievement. The states began the effort in the 1990s. Some did so quite rigorously with explicit achievement goals and meaningful sanctions. We have known for some time that states that held schools accountable for test score gains saw greater increases in their statewide achievement averages, as measured by NAEP, than states that merely tested students but did not attach

26. Adaptive assessments developed by the Northwest Education Association (NWEA) are used in 3,100 school districts nationwide, to cite only the most widely used example of this form of testing. See NWEA's website, www.nwea.org.

consequences to school performance.[27] More recent research has shown that states with serious accountability regimens also reduced their achievement gaps during the 1990s. At grade four in reading and math and grade eight in math the gap between students in the bottom and top 10 percent of the NAEP score distribution narrowed more in tough accountability states than in weak ones.[28]

NCLB holds the prospect of improving the results demonstrated by the states in the 1990s. By requiring all states to set annual achievement goals, rising over time to universal proficiency, and to implement a federally specified system of incentives and sanctions, NCLB promises to help all states become tough on accountability. To be sure, states have not responded to NCLB with equally tough systems, as the variation in standards makes clear. But the early evidence is that accountability under NCLB has produced gains. A study completed in late 2008, capturing as much of the NCLB era as possible, found that states that adopted consequential accountability systems made greater gains than states that did not.[29] The largest individual gains may be among students expressly targeted by the law—the ones most likely to be left behind. Through 2007, NAEP data indicate that the lowest 10 percent of all students have made large gains in math in grades four and eight, exceeding a grade equivalent in scale points. Reading gains were significant in grade four. These post-NCLB improvements were much greater than gains made by these students prior to NCLB.[30]

27. Eric A. Hanushek, "Impacts and Implications of State Accountability Systems," in John E. Chubb, ed. *Within Our Reach: How America Can Educate Every Child* (Stanford, CA: Hoover Institution Press, 2005), pp. 95–112.

28. Duffet, Farkas, and Loveless, *High Achieving Students.*

29. Tom S. Dee and Brian A. Jacobs, American Association of Policy and Management, Fall Conference, November 2008, Los Angeles.

30. The data on the differential gains of students in the top and bottom 10 percent of the NAEP achievement distribution by time period are from Duffet, Farkas and Loveless, *High Achieving Students.*

Gains were also made in the post-NCLB era by the top 10 percent of the NAEP achievement distribution. These gains too were greater than occurred during the 1990s when states often lacked strong accountability. The gains by the highest and the lowest achieving students may well have causes other than NCLB, but they are fully consistent with the way NCLB was intended to work. Importantly, the gains by the lowest students exceeded those of the highest students, reducing the achievement gap. The gains by the lowest students did not come at the expense of the highest students; both groups gained but at different rates. This is encouraging news because NCLB currently offers no incentive for achievement growth among the very top students, a problem we proposed to correct with our previous recommendation.[31]

The evidence suggests, then, that accountability, as a general proposition, is an effective means of improving school performance. The early evidence suggests that NCLB is enhancing accountability. We emphasize *early* because more time and research are needed to understand precisely how NCLB is influencing student achievement. But precise estimates aside, it is also clear that some elements of NCLB accountability are not working and should be fixed.

In particular, NCLB provides for an escalating series of sanctions from the first year of a school being in "needs-improvement" status, which occurs after missing AYP two consecutive years, to the sixth consecutive year of missing AYP, when a school is to be "restructured." The problem with the series of sanctions is that it applies to schools *regardless of why or by how much they miss AYP.*

31. The absence of a strong "robin hood effect" has also been found in research examining the progress of students close to proficiency, the so-called "bubble kids," on the verge or bubble of passing their state tests. There is little evidence that school efforts to help students closest to passing have shortchanged students above or below them. See, for example, Matthew G. Springer, "Do Schools Practice Educational Triage?" *Education Next* (Winter 2008, vol. 8, no. 1), pp. 75–79.

The greatest problem arises for schools that miss AYP for a single subgroup—which could be as small as twenty-five students. Those schools do not need the same strong medicine required by schools failing the majority of their students. The overkill that such schools face is not a small problem: upwards of half of all schools that fail to make AYP fail for subgroup reasons, and not for the performance of students overall. For example, in 2004–2005, 21 percent of all schools that failed to make AYP failed because of a single subgroup; another 19 percent failed because of two or more subgroups.[32] NCLB generates needless backlash from educators when it imposes this kind of unfairness.

The Department of Education recognizes this issue and in 2008 began a pilot for "differentiated accountability."[33] States could propose to the Department a regimen that distinguished degrees of failure and interventions customized to match the failure. Proposals could not allow backsliding on schools failing most seriously, and had to include provisions for restructuring those. As of January 2009, nine states were authorized to experiment with varying forms of differentiated accountability. We support these pilots. We believe that the federal government is ill equipped to specify exactly how schools should be improved and that NCLB should give more discretion to the states, which are closest to the problems. But the pilot does not go far enough, and NCLB should be amended to ensure that differentiated accountability gets the job done.

We propose that NCLB offer not infinite flexibility and differentiation, which the federal government would be burdened to oversee in any case. We propose a simplified system of differentiation. The failure to make AYP—redefined based on growth models—should

32. Institute of Education Sciences, *National Assessment of Title I*, p. 65.

33. U.S. Department of Education, "Differentiated Accountability: A More Nuanced Approach to Better Target Resources," March 2008.

be broken into two categories: "schoolwide improvement" needed and "limited improvement" needed. Schools that miss AYP for their entire population would go into the schoolwide category. Schools that miss for subgroups that represent less than *one-third* of all students tested would go into the limited category.[34] Schools would then face a simplified six-year regimen.

In year one of needs-improvement (year two of failing to make AYP), students in schools in both categories would be eligible to choose other schools *and* receive Supplementary Education Services (SES), both of which we propose to modify (as described below). Students would immediately benefit, and schools would have incentive to improve, to avoid the loss of the Title I funds used for these purposes. In year three of needs-improvement (a fourth consecutive year of not making AYP), schools in the schoolwide category would be required to work with states on "corrective action plans," which would need to address the widespread failure. Schools in the limited category would face no additional sanctions other than the continued loss of funds for choice and SES. In year four of needs-improvement, schools in the schoolwide category would need to plan for restructuring, which (as explained below) would be dramatically toughened. If AYP was missed for a sixth consecutive year (year five in needs-improvement status), a school with school-wide problems would have to restructure.

Schools in the limited category of improvement, were they to continue to fail their subgroups in year five status, would then be required to produce "limited corrective action plans," focused on the

34. The U.S. Department of Education improved subgroup accountability with regulations issued in November 2008 that specify how the statistical significance of subgroup size should be calculated and ensure thereby that schools are not held to account for subgroups too small to measure confidently their academic performance.

needs of their subgroups. States would be expected to monitor those plans and provide whatever support the state deemed appropriate. The federal government would help those schools by continuing to offer students tutoring and choice.

Classifying schools as needing limited improvement will become increasingly important as schools reach higher levels of proficiency. As schools strive to reach universal proficiency, the ultimate goal to which NCLB asks the nation to aspire, the percentages of students falling short of proficiency will decline and the likelihood that missing AYP will be only subgroup related will increase. As an ongoing proposition, we are recommending that schools that are succeeding with the vast majority of their students *not* face harsh and unnecessary measures from the federal government but be left to the care of the states—while students in these schools receive direct help from Washington in the form of tutoring and choice. Critics of NCLB have occasionally raised the specter of every school in America "failing" and facing restructuring in 2014, when universal proficiency is required. With differentiated accountability, most schools that fail to make AYP will be treated to only the modest remedies appropriate to their needs.

NCLB needs to recognize degrees of failure and needs to get the federal government out of the school improvement business, for which it is fundamentally ill equipped. At the same time, the federal government cannot give infinite latitude to states to hold schools accountable. A simplified regimen distinguishing massive failure from limited failure would offer ample flexibility while still ensuring that the most troubled schools are not tolerated forever.

One final thought: while the federal government is assuming an accountability role for which it is well suited, we recommend one additional role at which the federal government has historically excelled. Accountability requires transparency. School performance issues need to be clear before they can receive attention. NCLB requires states and school districts to post school report cards that convey test scores, additional information, and school improvement status. But the information—now in welcome abundance—can nevertheless be a challenge for parents, citizens, and others with an interest in school performance to access. The federal government has a strong track record as a repository of information and statistics on education and the gamut of policy fields.

We recommend that NCLB be revised to require the US Department of Education to maintain on its website a database of every public school in the nation, reporting each school's AYP and needs-improvement status. The database would not attempt to replicate the detail in school report cards. The federal database would simply ensure that the one piece of information that NCLB is all about—how successfully, or unsuccessfully, a school is helping students achieve reading and math proficiency—is easy for all Americans to access.

4. Students need a rich and rigorous curriculum to succeed in the twenty-first century, yet by focusing accountability on only reading and math, NCLB has discouraged curricular depth and breadth. NCLB should be amended to require that social science (specifically, history, civics, and geography) and science each be tested three times during the K–12 years. As with reading and math, tests should be based on explicit standards of the knowledge and skills that constitute proficiency at each grade level. Test scores should be reported to parents and communities in publicly accessible school report cards. States should be free to set their own standards in these subjects and scores should not count toward AYP. Accountability in these neglected subject areas will be enhanced by making performance transparent and,

we recommend, by requiring benchmarking of state test scores against NAEP.

Reading and math are foundation skills, and NCLB is right to make them the nation's top priorities. They are important in their own right but just as important in supporting other areas of education. Students cannot learn any other subject unless they can read effectively—and this means not only decoding and fluency but comprehension in all of its dimensions, from recall to analysis, inference, evaluation, and other higher order thinking skills. Math is similarly important. A range of technical disciplines such as physics, chemistry, engineering, and economics cannot even be approached by students unless they are well versed in mathematics.

But having the skill to learn other disciplines and actually learning them are two different things. The evidence is that American students are not learning subjects besides reading and math well at all. And unlike reading and math, where there is evidence of some improvement, in other subjects there is little or none. As we saw in the NAEP data, US student scores in history, civics, and science are abysmally low and generally stuck there. International data reinforce the finding that science scores are low, not just absolutely but relative to other nations as well.

The problem is not new. The poor state of scientific and historical knowledge has been clear in the data and recognized by reformers and policymakers since *A Nation at Risk*. The difference today is that our education policies may actually be exacerbating the problem. NCLB and the state accountability systems that preceded it have gotten the attention of our public schools in a very big way. School systems want their schools to satisfy state and federal achievement standards. Failure has become far too visible to accept, and the sanctions that accompany failure have become appropriately onerous. On the positive side, we must assume that schools appreciate the recognition that now comes with "making AYP," or gaining a high-status score in their state accountability systems—for example, earning an A in Florida's system. But for all the good that accountability is doing for reading and math, it is doing no favors for other subjects. Indeed, the evidence is that schools are devoting less time to teaching science, history, and the fine arts in order to give more time to reading and math.[35] Given this, it is something of a wonder that scores in other subjects have merely remained low and not declined further.

This is clearly not a situation that the United States should tolerate. Young people will not mature into productive citizens or leaders in the workplace of tomorrow if they do not understand science and technology or the history and politics of this country and the ever shrinking world they are entering. There is simply no disputing the importance of an education broad and rich in content. There is also ample reason to believe that learning other subjects does not compete with mastery of reading and math fundamentals. Substantial research demonstrates that reading skills cannot be developed without extensive exposure to the vocabulary, knowledge, and skills that are associated with reading, history, science, and other content areas.[36] Similarly, mathematics could be a dry and arcane subject without its application to other subjects to which students can relate. A well-planned curriculum can and should yield strong reading and math skills as well as rich content knowledge. These are not competing priorities.

35. See, for example, Sam Dillon, "Schools Cut Back on Subjects to Push Reading and Math," *New York Times* (March 26, 2006).

36. The evidence is best summarized in E.D. Hirsch, *The Knowledge Deficit: Closing the Shocking Education Gap for American Children* (Boston: Houghton, Mifflin, Harcourt, 2007).

With NCLB the nation has embraced the concepts of explicit standards and accountability to raise achievement. It is logical and even necessary to apply these concepts across the essential curriculum. To do otherwise is to give schools the wrong signal—that reading and math are vital and all else is secondary. Most nations have seen the merit of this and test all major content areas. Now that the United States, through NCLB, has proceeded down the path of standards and accountability, science and social science should be made an integral part of the program.

We propose that NCLB be amended to require testing of social science—meaning, US history, world history, civics, and geography—as well as science three times each: once in grades three through five, six through nine, and ten through twelve. NCLB already requires science testing in these grade spans. We recommend adding social science—as well as certain other measures to help the testing raise achievement in these areas. States already have academic standards for history and other social studies, as they have for science. Schools are supposed to be following them. NCLB can and should encourage this for the sake of student growth in these important fields. NCLB should never discourage attention to these fields by focusing too narrowly on reading and math.

We recommend that states be free to set their own social science and science standards. Currently, state standards vary widely in content and rigor. This is undesirable, but in our view not best addressed in the same fashion we recommend for reading and math—multistate consortia of standards and tests. Some of the state variation reflects legitimate differences of opinion about the sequencing of knowledge and skills or about points of emphasis, particularly in history. While we do think the nation should ultimately have national science and social science standards, we do not believe the time is now ripe for the federal government to promote or require their development. The nation should allow voluntary efforts by the states to develop better and more consistent standards to run their course.

We would ask that NCLB place only one requirement on the standards tested during each grade span. The tests must assess knowledge and skills across the full domain covered by state standards during a grade span, which should cover each field comprehensively. Science includes physical, life, and earth sciences—or later, physics, biology, and chemistry. History includes the United States and the rest of the world—from the twentieth century back to ancient times. Social science also includes civics, geography, and other subjects such as economics that we are not asking to be tested. If testing were annual, it would be possible to divide science and social science into annual chunks that could be taught and tested in specific grades, at state discretion. With only periodic testing, however, we are faced with a difficult choice—only test certain topics, just taught during the tested grade level, or test topics covered over multiple grade levels. Each approach has issues—the former leaving much valuable content unexamined and the latter requiring students to retain and accumulate knowledge and skills beyond the grade level when it was taught or most emphasized.

We believe the comprehensive approach, while most challenging to students and teachers, is the better approach by far. Our recommendation for testing science and social science, after all, is intended to reinforce the importance of the full curriculum. Let us not now devalue various areas of science and social science by inviting their omission from state assessments. Well constructed state assessments in science and social science will be able to test for recall of the essential knowledge that should be carried forward from one grade level to the next while also emphasizing science and social science skills that demand reasoning with facts supplied as part of the test. We stress the feasibility of this approach because we do not want to encourage a proliferation, for example, of US history tests that omit the rest of the social sciences, or life science assessments that leave out the rest of the hard sciences. Such an outcome could further distort the teaching of vital fields—something NCLB should, as we recommend, be striving to avoid.

Each state should be free to set science and social science standards, and the grade level scope and sequence of instruction to support them. We believe that states will voluntarily join forces to develop standards and the tests to support them to be efficient and to take advantage of shared viewpoints on how standards and tests should be crafted. NCLB should be written with the faith that voluntary efforts by the states will help the nation move toward common expectations about proficiency in science and social science. We would ask, however, that NCLB be revised to support these voluntary efforts with formal benchmarking of state tests. NAEP already has frameworks and national assessments in the fields we propose for state testing. NCLB should fund the extension of NAEP's state testing program to include science and social science. NCLB should then be modified to require NAEP benchmarking of state science and social science assessments. Having a common metric against which to evaluate state assessments will help states judge the rigor of their work and, we hope, improve assessments with time.

Last is the matter of accountability. Incentives and sanctions must be proportional to the ends in any accountability system. The United States has adopted an audacious goal of universal proficiency in reading and math, the subjects upon which the acquisition of all other academic knowledge and skills rest. Progress in these subjects is governed by demanding annual AYP targets and ever tougher sanctions. This regimen, amended as recommended above, is appropriate for the fundamentals of reading and math. But it is not for the rest of the curriculum. Accountability in social science and science should not be governed by AYP. States and the nation should want all students proficient in these subjects as well, but the federal government is not now in a position to say at what pace or by what means proficiency should be achieved. The urgency is also not quite as great as with the fundamentals of reading and math.

NCLB will substantially raise accountability for social science and science achievement by requiring their regular comprehensive testing and by shining the bright light of transparency upon them. States will not want their social science and science achievement regularly exposed as mediocre—by their own test scores and by NAEP benchmarking against national standards and other states. Schools will no longer be comfortable teaching reading and math and neglecting the rest of the curriculum. Frequent public reports of science and social science scores will make any neglect clear. Teaching these vital subjects will also improve literacy and numeracy. It is critical to strike an appropriate balance in any accountability system between the proverbial carrots and sticks. For science and social science, NCLB should trust and embrace the states as partners in defining a curriculum with the breadth and depth that the future clearly demands.

5. Information is a powerful force that can generate positive change without any government prescription. NCLB deserves credit for making school performance much more transparent to families and communities through annual school report cards with mandatory performance indicators and parental notification of school failure, among other measures. NCLB could do much better, however, by ensuring states provide the most valuable kinds of information, such as the effectiveness of individual teachers. NCLB should be amended to require states to build *comprehensive education information systems* that not only measure annual student academic growth but that link individual teachers, administrators, and other school attributes to student growth. Modest matching grants should be added to Title I to support state data systems. NCLB could make the most important determinants of student achievement much more transparent.

Perhaps the most powerful effect of NCLB, and of the state accountability systems that preceded it, is heightening awareness about school performance. A generation ago, parents, communities, the media, and even responsible authorities such as boards of education, did not have a clear idea how their schools were performing. Standardized tests were given largely to measure the performance of students, not schools. Measures were nationally norm referenced and drifted inevitably upward over time, creating a Lake Wobegon world in which every school was seemingly above average.[37] Measures were manipulated to improve appearances, as drop-out rates, long underestimated, notoriously illustrate. NCLB, picking up on the work of many states before it, has rapidly provided the nation with a uniform system of vastly better information about how schools are performing.

The information could be even better. This is particularly so for information on student achievement. Academic standards and criterion-referenced tests, now universal, have been a major step toward defining and gauging student achievement. Yet, as the discussion of growth models illustrates, the measurement of learning

37. Norm-referenced tests are not inherently weaker than criterion-referenced tests. Each is subject to manipulation and distortion. We only mean to call attention to the common misuses of norm-referenced tests, which dominated assessment prior to the 1990s.

requires more than knowing a school's or even a student's *level* of achievement. Learning is about acquiring *more* skills and knowledge. Measuring learning requires information about achievement *gains*. Schools should be accountable for helping students gain—or learn more each year.

As simple as this may seem in concept, it has its challenges in practice. Tests must be comparable year to year—so, for example, proficiency implies the same level of difficulty or mastery in grade five as in grade four. Test data must be saved year after year and matched student by student so that student gains can be calculated. Because students move around a lot, from school to school and district to district, the test data must be maintained at the state level. Then the gains of each student can be calculated year to year, as long as a student does not leave the state. Unfortunately, many states do not yet have the capacity to measure individual student gains year over year. Under NCLB states have only been testing consecutive grade levels three through eight since 2006. Prior to the late 1990s, many states left testing to school districts and testing companies. Currently, only fifteen states have growth model pilots approved by the US Department of Education. The main reason the rest of the states are not participating is that most of them do not have data systems that allow them to calculate individual student gains and estimate growth models that would permit growth to be a standard of accountability.[38]

The federal government could most swiftly accelerate the effective use of accountability if it could spur the development of comprehensive state student testing and information systems. We therefore recommend NCLB be amended to mandate that each state develop

38. A minimum of three consecutive years of student data are necessary to obtain quality growth measures.

a comprehensive education information system. The systems should be required to include unique identifiers for each student, so that gain scores can be calculated statewide, and all necessary analyses of student achievement can be carried out at the student level. The systems should also include standard requirements statewide for other student information of the sort normally carried in district student information systems: including all NCLB subgroup designations, classes enrolled in (for secondary students), graduation and postgraduation status, discipline record, and attendance. Most importantly, it should include designation of every student's teacher or teachers and building principal.

This last requirement cannot be emphasized enough. There is nothing more important to a child's achievement than quality instruction—and that depends most on the teacher doing the teaching. State data systems should not be permitted to omit linked identifiers for students and for teachers. Data systems with these features will make possible the calculation not only of student growth but the calculation of the effectiveness of teachers associated with the growth. There is much controversy about such linkages, and teacher unions are on record opposing them: they do not want the effectiveness of individual teachers calculated from test scores. Indeed, today only sixteen states permit teacher identifiers to be linked to student identifiers—and those are largely states where teacher unions are not highly influential.[39] Yet, besides student learning itself, there is nothing more important to make transparent than the effectiveness of the teachers—and principals—responsible for producing the learning. NCLB would advance school improvement immeasurably by simply shining a

39. See Terry M. Moe and John E. Chubb, *Liberating Learning: Technology, Politics and the Future of American Education* (San Francisco: Jossey-Bass, 2009), ch. 5.

bright light on the subject that until now has remained all too hidden from sight—true teacher quality.

Some will object that requiring comprehensive state data systems will add yet another "unfunded mandate" to NCLB. To be clear, the creation and maintenance of these data systems is essential for the implementation of academic growth models, which the states themselves have been demanding. Technology is making the systems ever easier and less expensive to implement. The federal government has already provided twenty-six states grants worth tens of millions of dollars each to develop longitudinal data systems. It is time that all states put adequate data systems promptly into place. We recommend the data systems be operational within two years of NCLB's reauthorization. We further recommend that NCLB authorize *one-to-one matching grants* good for two years to support the development or improvement of comprehensive data systems.[40] Quality achievement data are too important for improving achievement to be held up by financial squabbles. The costs are not that high and the return on investment—knowing whether students are learning more each year and whether teachers are really effective—is enormous.

6. Research has made abundantly clear that teachers are the most important school-based determinant of student achievement. Research has also demonstrated that traditional measures of teacher quality such as credentials and education have little or nothing to do with quality as measured by student achievement. NCLB's teacher quality provisions—"Highly Qualified

---

40. President Obama's "economic stimulus package" includes substantial funds for state data systems but does not require those systems include the features we deem essential to their effectiveness.

Teachers" (HQT)—are based on largely faulty credentialing premises and have been implemented in bad faith. NCLB should be amended to scrap its HQT provisions and replace them with incentive grants to states to pilot programs that seek to raise teacher effectiveness by measuring it directly with *value-added student achievement metrics* or other outcome-based measures and rewarding performance with financial incentives.

Research has taught us more about the effectiveness of teachers and teaching than any other factor influencing student achievement. The results are consistent and strong. Individual teachers have large effects on how much students learn. Estimates generally range from .25 to .50 standard deviations. Translated into test scores, a top quality teacher might have an effect of up to fifty national percentiles over a three-year period when compared to a low quality teacher. An excellent teacher can reliably move a below basic student to proficiency. Unfortunately, a poor teacher can reliably do the reverse. The effects of teachers have been so frequently demonstrated that it is fair to say knowledgeable policymakers do not question the point.[41]

The question is what to do about it. Conventional wisdom was once that teacher quality could be ensured through credentialing—earning

41. Estimates of teacher effects vary widely, but almost invariably show significant and substantial effects. At the upper end of estimated effects, see William L. Sanders and S. Horn, "Research Findings from the Tennessee Value Added Assessment System (TVAAS) Database: Implications for Educational Evaluation and Research," *Journal of Personnel Evaluation in Education* (1998, vol. 12, no. 3), pp. 247–56. More moderate but still substantial estimates are provided by Steve Rivkin and Eric A. Hanushek, "Teachers, Schools and Academic Achievement," *Econometrica* (2005, vol. 73, no. 2), pp. 417–458. Low but significant estimates are found in B. Nye and S. Konstantopoulos, "How Large are Teacher Effects?" *Educational Evaluation and Policy Analysis* (2004, vol. 26), pp. 237–58.

a bachelor's degree and a teaching certificate through a school of education and then greater knowledge and skill through master's degrees and doctorates. Degrees, credentials, and finally experience, were regarded as good measures of teacher quality. Teachers are universally compensated in public education based on these criteria. Yet research has shown for some time that education credentials predict nothing about student achievement. Experience counts for something but only for the first five years on the job.[42]

The reason for these negative findings is that the skills that distinguish effective teachers from ineffective ones are skills that can only be confidently demonstrated on the job: managing student behavior, using classroom time efficiently, motivating students to learn academic content, focusing lessons around clear objectives, providing students appropriate opportunities to practice and refine skills, offering useful feedback on student work, differentiating instruction to the learning needs of different students. The list goes on—with skill after skill that simply cannot be guaranteed by training outside the classroom. Teachers are all schooled in the best instructional practices in college, graduate school, and ongoing professional development workshops. But only some teachers are able to execute these practices effectively in the classroom. Credentials simply cannot predict who they will be.

42. The factors that predict and fail to predict teacher success have been the subject of more research than any other influence on student achievement. Representative studies include, Eric A. Hanushek, "Assessing the Effects of School Resources on Student Performance: An Update," *Educational Evaluation and Policy Analysis* (1997, vol. 19, no. 2), pp. 141–64; Daniel D. Goldhaber and Dominic J. Brewer, "Does Teacher Certification Matter? High School Teacher Certification Status and Student Achievement," *Educational Evaluation and Policy Analysis* (2000, vol. 22, no. 2), pp. 129-45; and Linda Darling-Hammond, "Teacher Quality and Student Achievement: A Review of State Policy Evidence," *Education Policy Analysis Archives* (2000, vol. 8, no. 1).

NCLB recognized that conventional measures of effectiveness did not determine quality, but it nonetheless took a credentialing route to improving teacher quality. NCLB requires that all public school teachers be "highly qualified" by 2006 (later delayed by the Department of Education to 2007) by doing the following: acquiring a traditional state teaching certificate *and* demonstrating subject matter competence. While there is limited research to support a relationship between subject matter expertise and teacher effectiveness among secondary teachers—for example, college math majors are more successful high school math teachers than non-math majors—the requirement has proven a very weak remedy for poor teacher quality.

First, the effects of subject matter competence have only been demonstrated for secondary teachers and not for elementary. Second, the estimated effects are small relative to the overall effects of teachers. Finally, NCLB only includes meaningful requirements for new teachers, who must either have a relevant college major or pass a subject matter competency test.[43] Veteran teachers can demonstrate their subject matter competence through HOUSSE (High Objective Uniform State Standard of Evaluation) procedures that states have used to declare all veterans highly qualified—based on training and experience. As a consequence, school districts now routinely report that nearly 100 percent of their teachers are "highly qualified" while large percentages of their schools are failing. This is untenable—and unacceptable.[44]

NCLB will never improve teaching if it sticks to its current approach. Teaching certificates simply do not predict quality. Subject area competence matters in some instances, but credentials do

43. Ibid.
44. Institute of Education Sciences, *National Assessment of Title I*, pp. 106–121.

not adequately measure it. NCLB should embrace instead what is well known about teacher effectiveness. It is the most important school-based determinant of student achievement; no other school-based factor comes close to a .25–.50 standard deviation influence. And, while it cannot be predicted by credentials, it can be measured on the job—where it is either demonstrated or not. With the advent of the annual testing of students, comprehensive student information systems, and identifiers linking students with their teachers, it has become possible to measure the influence of individual teachers on their students' learning, controlling for factors beyond a teacher's influence, such as poverty, family, a poor school environment, and more. In statistical terms, it is possible to measure a teacher's "value added," what the teacher added uniquely to the student's annual academic progress.

If schools have knowledge of each teacher's value added—or at least that of the teachers teaching tested subjects—the school can do much to improve. The school can provide extra support to teachers with low value-added scores. It can match high value-added teachers with teachers who are struggling to mentor and coach. It can match teachers with students with whom they are most successful. It can offer financial rewards to teachers with high value-added scores. Of course, as a last resort, a school can remove a teacher who provides no value added at all. A number of states and school districts have been experimenting with value-added teacher assessment—Tennessee, Florida, Denver, the District of Columbia, New York City, to name only the largest. There is no one best way to make it work. But it is the one best way conceptually to drive teacher quality—to measure it directly.

NCLB should promote this experimentation. To show the nation's commitment to high quality teaching, NCLB should be amended to *eliminate* the current highly qualified teacher requirements. If states wish to require certification and subject matter credentials, that is their prerogative. NCLB would already be amended to support value-added measurement by underwriting comprehensive state data systems. NCLB should additionally support teacher quality by offering states incentive grants for financing school districts that wish to implement value-added teacher measurement *and* a system of financial rewards to attract and retain teachers who demonstrate the ability to help their students achieve.

These systems must measure teacher effectiveness directly. If the systems also include teacher attributes, like subject matter competence, which can be shown to predict teacher effectiveness, so much the better. The key is teachers must be judged on their ability to raise achievement. That is what adding value is all about. To be clear, value-added measures need not, and should not, be the only measures of teacher effectiveness. Schools should also develop reliable tools for observing and gauging teacher behaviors that raise achievement. Such measures can and should be included in new systems for judging teacher quality. But new systems must attempt to evaluate teacher effectiveness directly, by estimating teacher effects on student achievement. NCLB ought to encourage schools to do this and reward it. In the process, the nation will learn much more about how best to use value-added measurement. NCLB should be encouraging the nation to learn.

7. NCLB's school choice provision is not working. Students are not using it, and schools are not concerned about losing students if they fail them. The premise of choice is nonetheless sound. Ample evidence indicates that choice outside of NCLB has raised achievement, and it is sound policy to offer students in failing schools a way out. The problem is NCLB offers too few choices with too little time to access them. NCLB should be amended

to expand the choices available to families to include *any public school* in their district, *regardless of the receiving school's AYP status*, any public school in *any other school district in the state*, and *any private school* in the district. NCLB should also try to expand the availability of charter schools in districts with especially high rates of failure by offering start-up grants. Finally, NCLB should keep the choice option open to families for a full year after eligibility first occurs.

The efficacy of school choice has slowly but surely become less debatable. A generation ago, the ideas that public schools would not all be under the control of local school boards, or that families could routinely choose their schools, or that schools ought to compete for students and resources were highly controversial. Today, forty states plus the District of Columbia permit public charter schools. Over four thousand charter schools serve more than one million school children nationwide.[45] Charter schools are carefully monitored by authorizing agencies, such as public universities and not-for-profit institutes, which provide tough accountability and willingly close down ineffective charter schools. Many urban school districts have embraced charter schools as part of their reform strategy. New York City, which had few charter schools only a few years back, now has over seventy-five.

Research has now consistently shown that charter schools are not, contrary to early fears, "creaming" the most able students from traditional public schools. Charters tend to serve students who are disproportionately disadvantaged, belong to racial minorities, and

45. In 2008 charter schools numbered 4,568 and enrolled 1,341,687 students, numbers that continued to grow without interruption at about 10 percent per year. Center for Education Reform, *Annual Survey of America's Charter Schools 2008* (Washington, D.C.: October 2008).

were relatively unsuccessful in their original public school, if they began in one. Research on the academic impact of charter schools has been more controversial, but the strongest studies scientifically indicate that students in charter schools are gaining more than comparable students in traditional schools. Research also indicates that charter schools can help all public schools improve. Traditional public schools tend to raise their test scores more rapidly when charter schools present competition for them.[46]

Even private school choice has made headway. Once a virtual taboo, private school choice was given legitimacy with the Supreme Court's decision in 2002 that private school vouchers did not necessarily violate the Constitutional separation of church and state.[47] Modest private school voucher programs now serve high poverty students in Cleveland, Milwaukee, and Washington, DC. These supplement larger philanthropically funded choice programs offering private school choice to economically disadvantaged students. Research on these programs remains controversial. But the general takeaway is that certain students—African Americans most consistently—are learning more in private schools than in public; no research suggests that students are fairing worse for choosing.[48]

46. See most recently the methodologically "gold standard" report on charter schools, Caroline M. Hoxby and Sonali Murarka, *New York City's Charter Schools Overall Report* (Cambridge, MA: New York City Charter School Evaluation Project, July 2007). More broadly, see Caroline M. Hoxby, "Does Competition among Public Schools Benefit Students and Taxpayers?" *American Economic Review*, 2000; and Paul T. Hill, *Charter Schools against the Odds* (Stanford, CA: Hoover Institution Press, 2006).

47. Zelman v. Simmons-Harris, 536 U.S. 639, 652 (2002); David Stout, "Public Money Can Pay Religious-School Tuition, Court Rules," *New York Times* (June 27, 2002).

48. William G. Howell and Paul E. Peterson, *The Education Gap: Vouchers and Urban Schools*, Revised Edition (Washington, D.C.: Brookings Institution, 2006).

Finally, private schools are proving a popular choice for special needs students in many places, including a voucher program in Florida— the McKay scholarships—serving over seven thousand students.[49]

Choice has proven popular with parents, particularly in the inner cities where public schools often struggle and personal financial limitations do not make private schools or a move to the suburbs feasible. Politically, school choice now enjoys support not only from the business community, a powerful early advocate that appreciates the free-market logic of choice, but from advocates for disadvantaged populations.[50] Charter schools, despite lingering opposition from the education establishment, are supported by both Republicans and Democrats—including President Barack Obama.

Choice is not without issues, to be sure. More research is clearly needed to understand the conditions under which choice is more or less effective. Expansion of charter options is still routinely opposed by teacher unions and boards of education. Nevertheless, choice has become an appealing and acceptable reform option, especially for students stuck in chronically underperforming schools.

NCLB embraces choice by allowing students in schools in needs-improvement status (failing to make AYP two years running) to choose another public school. This is a good idea: economically disadvantaged students in failing schools deserve an alternative while their school is trying to improve—which it may never do. Schools should not be able to count on their enrollments and funding no

49. Paul E. Peterson, ed. *Reforming Education in Florida: A Study Prepared by the Koret Task Force on K–12 Education*, (Stanford, CA: Hoover Institution Press, 2006).

50. On public opinion on school choice and vouchers, see Terry M. Moe, *Schools, Vouchers, and the American Public* (Washington, D.C.: Brookings Institution, 2001). Most recently, see Howell, West and Peterson, "The 2008 Education Next-PEPG Survey of Public Opinion."

matter how badly they perform. But choice is simply not working for NCLB. Only about 1 percent of eligible students have chosen another school.[51] The lack of choosing is not because failing schools are improving so rapidly that families are content to stay. Research indicates two problems. The first is that NCLB only permits families to select from public schools that are making AYP themselves and are in the same district as the school that is failing. Such schools are often few and far between in major school districts. Families may need to bus their kids miles and miles across town to reach a school eligible to receive students. The second reason is that school districts have been slow to facilitate choice by eligible families— failing to provide timely notice to families or to explain the benefits of changing schools—preferring not to spend Title I funds on the potential costs of choice such as transportation.

The US Department of Education is taking important steps to remedy the second problem. In regulations issued in October 2008, the Department now requires districts to notify families of their eligibility for choice at least fourteen days before a new school year begins, using preliminary test score data to make the deadline if necessary. The Department is also requiring that districts communicate clearly to families the benefits of choice and that they post permanently on their website schools that are eligible to lose and receive students.[52] These are helpful measures, but the key problem will not be remedied by them.

Choice is not working for NCLB because the law provides too few choices. We recommend that NCLB be amended to offer more

51. Comprehensive data, reflecting national samples of districts, are several years old. See Institute of Education Sciences, *National Assessment of Title I*, pp. 87–104. Anecdotal reports since the last comprehensive assessment continue to convey very low levels of participation.

52. Regulations were issued October 28, 2008. See www.ed.gov.

schools of choice. Specifically, we recommend that any regular or charter public school, *regardless of AYP status*, be eligible to receive choice students. Schools fail to make AYP for many reasons, as we have seen. Families ought to be able to size up schools and make changes even if their choice is a school that has some problems. Obviously, a school that has failed only a single small subgroup could hold much better prospects for students than a massively failing school would. Schools with only "limited" needs-improvement status, as we recommend, may often be better options than schools with "schoolwide" needs-improvement status—but the former are not now available for choosing. NCLB should recognize that schools fail by degrees and leave it to families to decide whether an alternative is superior for their child.

Choice options should also include schools in every other public school district in a state. Education is a state responsibility and school districts operate at the discretion of the respective states. States govern the access that students have from one district to another, and some states already give students the option of transferring across district lines, subject to the approval of the receiving district. NCLB ought to make this practice universal—for students in schools eligible for choice. Receiving schools would be paid the full per pupil funding for the transferring student, including federal, state, and local dollars. Chosen schools would be required to follow current practice under NCLB of accepting all eligible students, if space is available.[53] Receiving schools would be under no obligation to expand their capacity. Essentially, receiving schools

53. The constitutionality of this recommendation would need to be tested as it may be proscribed by the Supreme Court's historic ruling against "metropolitan" desegregation plans in Milliken v. Bradley 418 U.S. 717 (1974). Constitutionality could always be ensured, however, by making participation by receiving districts voluntary.

would have the opportunity to accept and help modest numbers of out-of-district students and take up their own financial slack with revenue otherwise unavailable to them—a win-win for transferring students and receiving schools. As a practical matter, this option will tend to appeal only to students living near the borders of school systems and willing to accept significant travel time to school. Sending districts would be required to offer transportation to district borders. Receiving districts would assume transportation responsibility from that juncture.

Imperfect as these additional school options may be—with the defects of not making AYP or requiring travel to another district—they offer clear improvements to students stuck in schools performing poorly. These options are within easy reach, and NCLB should endorse and require them. NCLB should also look to create entirely new schools as options. Charter schools have become commonplace in public education, especially in the nation's major cities. Yet charter schools are not as widespread as they might be, limited by state authorizing legislation that often fails to provide funding for their facilities, provides them less funding per pupil than traditional public schools, or outright restricts their number. NCLB cannot override state charter policy, but NCLB can and should spur charter school development by helping overcome the financial obstacles to starting charter schools. NCLB already offers charter schools as a choice to students in eligible schools. NCLB should beef up this option, as charter schools are the most promising means of expanding the supply of public schools near ones that are failing.

NCLB should be amended to offer start-up grants for state-approved entities wishing to launch charter schools in the districts with the greatest academic need. Districts should be targeted for charter school grants if as a whole they are not making AYP or if one-third of their schools are not making AYP, thereby limiting traditional-school choices. Grants should cover costs such as the salaries of a principal and business manager for a start-up year, lease or mortgage payments for up to one preopening year, and core curriculum and technology costs not covered by state budgets for all first-year students. In most states these new grants would only begin to level the playing field with the funding of traditional public schools—and not provide charters an advantage. Once open, charter schools would need to survive on the funding provided by their states and, of course, pass muster with the families free to choose or reject them and the testing systems that hold all public schools accountable.

The above recommendations will significantly expand the supply of public schools. But, in our view, NCLB should do *everything* possible to ensure that students in schools that are not serving them effectively have meaningful choices. That means every quality option should be made available. We therefore recommend private schools also be eligible to receive choice students. Many private schools make it their mission to serve disadvantaged students and could be a helpful safety valve for students needing a change. Private schools would have to accept per pupil public funding as tuition in full; no additional tuition could be charged. Private schools would also need to join state testing programs, so that their academic performance was transparent. Private school choice would of course need to be acceptable under state constitutions; in some cases it is not. The goal here, to be clear, is not to promote private education or to threaten public education. It is simply and urgently to ensure that students in failing schools have ample options and do not have to wait around while their school is fixed.

With this expanded universe of choices, we recommend one important procedural amendment. We recommend that the choice option be available for a year after it goes into effect, even if the school makes AYP. Fourteen days of notice is not enough for families to decide to change schools before a school year begins. Families need to be thoughtful about their choices, and providing a year to exercise choice can only make the process more intelligent.

8. Tutoring students individually or in small groups is one of the most effective and well established means of raising achievement. NCLB recognizes this and offers tutoring—or Supplementary Education Services (SES)—to students in schools that need improvement. It is a sensible and practical solution—that, unfortunately, is not working as well as it could nor reaching as many students as it should. As with choice, school districts have been reluctant SES participants, impeding the access of private tutors that the law correctly hoped to make available to disadvantaged families and arguing that districts can help their students more effectively and less expensively than private tutors. NCLB should be amended to offer SES services to students sooner—in year one of needs-improvement—and to make the market for SES work more effectively: districts and states (for the benefit of rural districts) should be allowed to be SES providers regardless of AYP status. Simultaneously, NCLB should guarantee private providers access to student information, school facilities, and applications for eligible students, and opportunity to communicate to families—so that districts, states, and private providers can compete for parental services on a level playing field. Districts should lose the right to provide SES if they fail to comply. To help ensure academic quality, NCLB should require that districts collect and distribute to eligible families audited pre/post assessment data on all providers, public and private.

Every year millions of American parents dip into their pockets to pay for tutoring for their children. It may be for basic skills that their children are struggling with in the primary grades, or acceleration and enrichment as children master the regular school curriculum, or help preparing for college entrance exams in high school. In Japan, the vast majority of parents pay for after-school tutoring—juku or "cram schools"—to give their children a leg up in the competition for seats in the best secondary schools.[54] Parents in the United States and around the world make these investments because, widespread experience suggests, tutoring works.

Research confirms the judgment of parents.[55] Small group and individual instruction are effective because, properly conducted, they enable very focused teaching, assessment, and reteaching, until students master or at least significantly improve the skills being tutored. Tutoring has become a $2 billion industry in the United States, entirely on the strength of parental willingness to pay. Substantial and longstanding companies such as Kaplan, Sylvan, Princeton Review, Huntington, and others invest in the development of ever more competitive and effective programs. With the Internet, companies around the world, often employing highly educated tutors from India and China, instruct American students online. This dynamic market speaks to the efficacy and promise of tutoring for helping students learn.[56]

54. The classic study is Harold W. Stevenson and James W. Stigler, *The Learning Gap: Why Our Schools Are Failing and What We Can Learn from Japanese and Chinese Education* (New York: Simon and Schuster, 1994).

55. On the effectiveness of various types of tutoring, see U.S. Department of Education, Institute of Education Sciences, National Center for Education Statistics, *What Works Clearing House.*

56. Tim Wiley, *Instruction for Hire: A Survey of the Private Tutoring Market* (Boston: Eduventures), January 2007. The growth rate in private tutoring is expected to pick up as home Internet connectivity becomes more universal and parent comfort with international tutors grows through experience. See also Jason Overdorf, "Tutors Get Outsourced," *Business 2.0* (August 2006), p. 32.

The tutoring market holds out promise for some students, but private tutoring is purchased largely by families with middle-class incomes and above. Low-income families, whose kids could certainly benefit from private tutoring, generally cannot afford to pay for it—until NCLB. In a bold stroke on behalf of equity, the act proclaimed that what is plainly good enough for middle-class children ought to be available to children not so advantaged. But as with other noble initiatives undertaken by NCLB, its aspirations did not adequately anticipate its realities.

The SES program, which offers private tutoring to low-income students in schools failing to make AYP, serves no more than 20 percent of eligible students and has become a major source of controversy.[57] School districts feel that private providers are often too expensive and unaccountable and would prefer to provide tutoring themselves. Even though NCLB increased Title I funding nearly 100 percent over its first eight years, many districts would prefer not to have to reserve 20 percent of all Title I dollars for school choice and SES, as required by NCLB. Some private providers have found that offering SES is not feasible logistically and have pulled out of the market. Private providers cannot afford to set up private tutoring centers, given the uncertainty of the marketplace, and parents cannot easily transport their children to tutoring centers in any case. Rural students are too geographically dispersed to be served profitably by private providers if they have to reach students one by one. School districts have impeded access to their students by private providers and have made minimally acceptable efforts in many cases to inform parents of their eligibility.

57. Institute of Education Sciences, *National Assessment of Title I*, pp. 87–104. For a discussion of the controversy, see Paul E. Peterson, "A Conflict of Interest: District Regulation of School Choice and Supplemental Services," in Chubb, *Within Our Reach*, pp. 141–72.

These problems and others were difficult to anticipate when NCLB was written. Ample experience now indicates that SES can be made to work. SES is based on sound principles: tutoring and small group instruction can be very effective, and competition among providers should drive improvements in quality. Some critics of SES would like it eliminated altogether, or limited to district-provided tutoring. There is no basis in theory or fact for such a position. SES absolutely needs to be improved. We recommend the following:

First, NCLB should be amended to allow all school districts to become providers of SES. NCLB currently bans districts from offering SES themselves if the district has failed to make AYP districtwide. This is a wildly unpopular provision among district officials and boards who do not appreciate being told they cannot serve their own students when they remain accountable for their achievement. The Department of Education has granted waivers to a few large districts, most visibly Chicago, which objected to the prohibition. This precedent should be followed. Districts are indeed accountable for achievement as gauged by AYP and, as we explain below, should be accountable for achievement in any tutoring program they might operate. Districts should have the opportunity to look for creative and effective ways to offer SES. This might include contracting with proven private tutoring companies to serve students on the district's behalf, and NCLB should not want to preclude this possibility.

Second, states and intermediate administrative units (serving multiple school districts) should be eligible to provide SES. This provision is necessary in particular to help reach students in rural areas. Because of the low concentrations of eligible students in rural areas, they sometimes do not provide a sufficient critical mass to attract private tutoring companies or even to support a district program. States and intermediate units would have the scale to make rural service provision more economical.

Third, with public providers fully eligible to offer tutoring, SES should then be further amended to guarantee there is ample private competition to ensure all providers are offering the best value to families for the federal dollars expended. NCLB currently makes it too easy for districts to block or impede private tutors from serving families. The biggest roadblocks are access to facilities and access to families. The most efficient and family-friendly means to offer SES is at school sites. Students can quickly transition at the end of the day from their regular school program to tutoring. Teachers at the sites become readily available and knowledgeable tutors for districts or private providers. Transportation from school to tutoring site is not a problem. Private providers have frequently struggled with districts for ready access to school facilities—which districts use with impunity to provide tutoring themselves, a monopolistic practice if ever there was one.

NCLB should be amended to apply the same rules of facility access to all providers, including school districts, intermediate units, and states. The law should specify a minimum number of students signed up for services as a common threshold for access to be granted—perhaps ten students. Similarly, the public providers must observe along with all providers the same rules for accessing families. The district must provide common opportunities for families to learn about private choices and about district options. Districts may not recruit students during school assemblies and then force private firms to recruit off of school premises. The procedure must be neutral as well in the process for selecting a provider, public or private.

Fourth, to help ensure a level playing field, NCLB should require states to maintain a database of all students eligible to receive SES services each year. The data base should provide names and addresses of families so that tutoring providers can contact families to describe their services, independent of district procedures for informing families and linking providers to them. Providers would be subject to state approval, as they are now, to receive student eligibility information from the state. Providers should also be prohibited by law from selling the lists or using them for any purpose other than offering SES enrollment to families. Asking the state to become an alternative source of information about student eligibility is a critical check on the willingness of districts to compete fairly.

Fifth, in an overarching attempt to create a fair market for SES, NCLB should ask districts to abide by a simple rule in structuring their SES program. The federal government cannot and should not attempt to prescribe the ideal conditions for a vital market in SES services for every local community. The beauty of federalism, and fifteen thousand school districts enabled by it, is the opportunity for experimentation. NCLB should encourage districts and providers to craft the most effective and efficient market for tutoring students possible. In doing so, NCLB should require that districts adhere to one general principle: whatever opportunities the district provides itself to access families, students, and teachers, to provide SES, it must also offer to all bona fide private providers. If a district materially violates this principle, NCLB should provide as sanction that the district lose its right to be an SES provider itself. It is a delicate and some would say impossible proposition for a district to both regulate and provide SES. NCLB needs to recognize this and take the serious steps outlined here to help make those conflicting roles work together.

Sixth, NCLB should require and audit evidence that tutoring programs, public and private, are effective. This is not easy from a technical standpoint, as no one test will work nationally, and different tutoring programs will be aimed at different academic skills. We recommend that tutoring companies be required to administer pre- and postprogram assessments and the average improvement scores be published on district Web sites along with other program characteristics.[58] We further recommend that states make available through their to-be-developed item banks pre- and postprogram assessments for the most important reading and math skills as articulated by their own standards. The recommended voluntary national standards and tests should also make available such assessments.

Finally, given the benefits that SES can provide to students immediately, we recommend the service be made available a year sooner than it is currently. The new NCLB ought to offer SES to low-income students in schools in the first year of needs-improvement—the same as school choice. SES has the clear and ready potential to help disadvantaged students achieve. It should be accelerated. But to work, it will require good faith effort to create a fair marketplace of providers, competing to do their best for students who without NCLB could never receive such services. The Department of Education will need to be vigilant that districts do not reestablish the monopolistic practices that until now have limited the access of low-income parents to private tutors. By establishing in legislation the conditions that the SES market must satisfy, NCLB can go a long way to ensuring that SES promotes education equity, as surely it should.

9. Some schools are in fact too bad for any child to have to attend. NCLB recognized this with its call for "restructuring" of schools in year six of needs-improvement. Restructuring has had a very mixed track record, however. Partly, this is due to the undifferentiated group

---

58. The averages could be reported as z-scores (standard deviation units) to allow comparisons among providers, addressing a technical issue that, left unresolved, precludes parents from comparing the results of providers.

of schools that may find themselves chronically missing AYP—some massively deficient, others barely missing—and the reluctance of states to force all schools to take the same drastic measures. Yet it is clear that some states have simply taken a more lax approach to failure than others. NCLB is partly to blame for this state of affairs because its restructuring requirements are vague. NCLB should be amended so that with its new differentiated accountability system, only massively deficient schools are identified in year six as requiring restructuring. Those schools should have but three well-defined restructuring options: change the school's governance by becoming a charter school; delegate management of the school to an external manager, either not-for-profit or for-profit; or make a wholesale change of school staff, meaning the principal and 100 percent of all teachers—no wiggle room.

At the end of all of the measures outlined thus far, restructuring becomes a straightforward necessity. NCLB is built on a sound foundation. We have recommended the following to strengthen that foundation:

+ Raising academic standards
+ Focusing the measurement of achievement on growth
+ Differentiating accountability to match consequences with needs
+ Broadening the tested curriculum to include science and social science
+ Building information systems to facilitate more intelligent accountability
+ Encouraging teachers to be supported and rewarded based on their actual effectiveness
+ Offering effective choice
+ Offering effective tutoring

If after all of these measures are employed to improve a school and it continues to fail schoolwide, as defined above, the school truly ought to be closed or changed fundamentally. There appears to be widespread agreement among policymakers that some schools are just too ineffective to ask students to attend them. When NCLB was passed, there was consensus that if, after all reasonable efforts to improve a school and raise achievement have been exhausted, a school is still not going in the right direction, a fundamentally new direction is needed.

The original law called this new direction restructuring and tried to specify reforms that would amount to fundamental change. Some of the approaches specified, such as converting a school to a charter and removing its governance from the school district, were and remain potentially fundamental. A new governing arrangement would likely yield very different decisions about how a school is staffed, what its education program should be, and how it should be run. If it were a charter, it would also have to worry about how to attract students and keep them enrolled, which might further encourage the school's improvement. Another NCLB restructuring option was contracting a school's management to a private company. This too has obvious potential to promote fundamental change. Like a charter board, a private manager would have latitude and incentive to make tough decisions and work aggressively for improvement.

Other restructuring options were vaguer, calling for unspecified program changes, staff changes, and measures tougher *sounding* than corrective action but little more. There is little formal research or data on the success of restructuring. But Department of Education oversight has identified restructuring compliance as a major area of concern. Clearly, some states have asked for relatively little of schools in restructuring while others have demanded more. The

Department has recently sought to improve restructuring with regulations requiring states to demonstrate that their restructuring requirements are materially different from and tougher than their corrective action requirements. We applaud the Department for recognizing the problem, but we think this regulatory approach comes up short. It keeps the Department in the business of judging the adequacy of school improvement plans, for which it inherently has little capacity. These are local matters. It also imposes restructuring requirements on schools that may not be failing enough to warrant it.

Our solution is twofold. First, NCLB should be amended to incorporate differentiated consequences, as described above. Only schools failing to make AYP schoolwide for six consecutive years would face the ultimate sanction. This is a very long time to tolerate abject failure. There should be little dispute that such schools need fundamental reform.

Second, the restructuring reforms should leave little discretion as to what type of change NCLB requires. Restructuring is for those schools that have been unable to make the changes necessary, given a long period of time, to become schools worthy of students attending. Restructuring should do everything possible to ensure those difficult and long overdue changes get made. This is best accomplished by putting different people in charge of the schools or changing completely the people in the schools. NCLB should therefore be amended to offer schools but three narrowly worded fundamental reforms: (1) becoming a charter school, subject to different governance and free to make wholesale changes in program, personnel, and operations; (2) becoming managed under contract by a private for-profit of not-for-profit management organization, changing the school's day-to-day oversight and creating the opportunity to overhaul programs, personnel, and operations;

or (3) changing the principal and 100 percent of the instructional staff—which while leaving the school under the governance of the school district will change day-to day-management and service to students.

Each of these approaches has real potential to set chronically failing schools in a new direction. NCLB should, in the end, make explicit that the time eventually comes when schools must make tough choices and change.

10. Achievement is too important to every child and to the nation to be viewed as anything but urgent. There is enough known about teaching and schooling to believe that most students can achieve reasonable grade level standards. NCLB set an ambitious goal of universal proficiency by 2014. That goal should not be changed—unless a state is willing to adopt the new voluntary national standards of college and career readiness or demonstrate that its own standards satisfy those rigorous conditions. If a state does adopt new standards, we propose extending the deadline by six years, half the timeline set when NCLB was adopted, requiring universal proficiency by 2020.

The final lesson for policymakers is straightforward. The nation has been making progress in reading and math since the 1990s. Gains in achievement and reductions in achievement gaps, inadequate though they may be, represent clear progress—and increasingly clear evidence that strategies embodied in NCLB are having the right effect. We know from substantial research into NCLB's various components—whether it is choice or teacher quality or tutoring or any of its other key elements—that NCLB is based on sound strategies. These strategies can and should be improved, as we have outlined. Doing so should increase and accelerate their positive effects on achievement. Policymakers should aim to reform and reauthorize NCLB as fast as possible, ideally during the 2009 legislative session.

In acting swiftly, Congress and the new administration should strive to keep one element of NCLB firmly in place. The 2014 deadline for universal proficiency, set by NCLB in 2002, is often criticized as unrealistic. States are currently far from achieving it. States set annual proficiency goals—known as Annual Measurable Objectives (AMOs) in the law—that leave much of the big improvements in achievement for the final years before 2014. It is easy to predict a train wreck not far down the road as huge numbers of schools fail to make AYP and the Department of Education is overwhelmed with petitions for relief from sanctions. Indeed, this task force warned of such an outcome in an analysis of NCLB in its earliest days.[59]

The 2014 deadline should not be relaxed—at least not now, and certainly not without conditions. The close proximity of this deadline represented a moral commitment when it was adopted in 2002. The nation should not require more time than the full twelve years of a school career to guarantee every child a good education. Many states and school districts have taken the challenge seriously and worked hard to improve. It would be unfair to places that might come genuinely close to the 2014 goal to relax the goal for others. The 2014 target also keeps the pressure on states and districts to work with increasing urgency, under an improved NCLB, to do the best things possible for their students. If the deadline needs to be relaxed, let it be only under conditions that make waiting additional years clearly worthwhile.

We think holding firm is the right thing to do, as a matter of moral purpose and a matter of good policy. But we also believe

59. Chubb, ed., *Within Our Reach.*

having standards worth achieving is vital. It is no victory when states with low standards declare themselves 100 percent proficient by dropping their standards to the most basic level. Indeed, we think the danger of this is the most important issue facing NCLB, and we devoted our first recommendation to it. NCLB must clarify what it means to be proficient in the twenty-first century. What is the common core of knowledge and skills that all students must have when they leave high school if they are to have a chance at a productive life free of poverty and subsistence living?

We defined this core as one that provides for reading and math skills sufficient to ensure college and career readiness. Such standards will be higher than those set by most states today. Yet they should not be so high that it is unreasonable to expect all children to master them—if they receive a decent education. Yes, there may be students with special needs or just learning English who may have to meet alternative standards. NCLB already makes fair and ample allowances for them.

As a technical matter, NCLB must acknowledge that "universal" may not mean precisely 100 percent of all nonexempt students in every school achieve proficiency: statistical confidence will require schools to meet thresholds less than 100 percent. Safe harbor provisions properly in NCLB already allow schools to continue to avoid needs-improvement status if they reduce their nonproficient performers by 10 percent a year—approaching 100 percent but never quite getting there. We have recommended further differentiating accountability to keep schools with "limited" improvement needs to avoid the toughest sanctions indefinitely—again promoting tolerance of certain shortfalls of universality. Dare we say it, "universal" may, as a practical matter, mean "only" 90–95 percent of all American youngsters being required to achieve the new core standards. This is an audacious goal nonetheless and one that in its clarity and openness about its aims should not be dismissed with the cynicism sometimes attendant on NCLB: universal proficiency is not ridiculous. The United States is right to define it and insist upon it.

Properly defined, universal proficiency will be a serious and worthy challenge for our education system to pursue. It is our hope that most if not all states will sign up for the challenge, join state consortia, and help the nation define, benchmark, and validate the high standards the nation requires. For those that do so, and create standards and tests that match the aspirations that the nation has expressed through NCLB, more time should be granted to achieve them.

There is no magic number. NCLB originally gave states twelve years to reach full proficiency—symbolically corresponding to a student's time in school. States have made progress already, and with an improved NCLB, progress should accelerate. The nation's young people, particularly the most disadvantaged, need better schools and higher achievement immediately. We suggest for states that are willing to adopt new core standards, an additional 6 years—half the original timeline—be provided. If the pressure remains on all states to achieve their current goals by 2014, or reach more worthy ones six years further on, the nation could, by 2020, offer all children an education they deserve. We have learned enough to do it. The time to do it is now.

About the Author

John E. Chubb is chief development officer and co-founder of EdisonLearning, a company that for nearly twenty years has partnered with public school districts and charter school boards nationwide to provide innovative schools and education programs, with a focus on disadvantaged students. Dr. Chubb is also a distinguished visiting fellow at the Hoover Institution at Stanford University and a member of the Koret Task Force on K-12 Education. He has previously served as a senior fellow at the Brookings Institution and faculty member at Stanford University.

Dr. Chubb's research focuses on student achievement, school choice, education technology, and education policy. He is the author of numerous books, including *Liberating Learning: Technology, Politics, and the Future of American Education* (Jossey-Bass, 2009), with Terry M. Moe; *Within Our Reach: How America Can Educate Every Child* (Hoover, 2005); and *Politics, Markets, and America's Schools* (Brookings, 1990). His numerous articles and professional papers have appeared in the *New York Times*, the *Wall Street Journal*, *Education Next*, the *Brookings Review*, and the *American Political Science Review*, among others, and many edited volumes.

Dr. Chubb has also served as an advisor to the White House, the U.S. Department of Education, state governments, and various education organizations. He holds a Ph.D. from the University of Minnesota and an A.B. *summa cum laude* from Washington University in St. Louis, both in political science.

ABOUT THE HOOVER INSTITUTION
TASK FORCE ON K–12 EDUCATION

The Task Force on K–12 Education is a top-rate team of education experts brought together by the Hoover Institution at Stanford University, with the support of the Koret Foundation and other foundations and individuals, to work on education reform. The primary objectives of the task force are to gather, evaluate, and disseminate existing evidence in an analytical context, and analyze reform measures that will enhance the quality and productivity of K–12 education.

The Task Force on K–12 Education includes some of the most highly regarded and best known education scholars in the nation. Most are professors at leading universities and many have served in various executive and advisory roles for federal, state, and local governments. Their combined expertise represents over 300 years of research and study in the field of education. Current members of the task force are John E. Chubb, Williamson M. Evers, Chester E. Finn Jr., Eric A. Hanushek, Paul T. Hill, Caroline M. Hoxby, Tom Loveless, Terry M. Moe, Paul E. Peterson, Diane Ravitch, and Herbert J. Walberg.

The eleven-member task force forms the centerpiece of the Hoover Institution's Initiative on American Educational Institutions and Academic Performance. In addition to producing original research, analysis, and recommendations in a growing body of work on the most important issues in American education today, task force members serve as editors, contributors, and members of the editorial board of *Education Next: A Journal of Opinion and Research*, published by the Hoover Institution.

www.hoover.org/taskforces/taskforces/education

Index

academic achievement, 7–15; above proficiency level, 27–30; adequate yearly progress in, 21, 26–31. *See also* adequate yearly progress; below basic level of, 2n1, 8–9; growth models on, 27–29, 45; in higher education, 10–11; of highest achieving students. *See* highest achieving students; impact of NCLB on, ix, 13–15, 14n16; international assessment of, 1n1, 7n4, 9–11; of lowest achieving students, 13–14, 33; NAEP reports on, 7–14. *See also* National Assessment of Education Progress; public information available on, in comprehensive state systems, 43–47; and readiness for college or career, 10–11. *See also* college and career readiness; school accountability for, 4–5, 31–37. *See also* accountability; in science and history, 14–15, 37–43; state standards on, 1n1, 17–26. *See also* state standards on academic achievement; subgroup problems in, 34, 35–36; Supplementary Education Services for assistance in, 35, 60–66; and teacher effectiveness, 47–52; universal proficiency goal and deadline on, vii, 3, 21, 27, 36, 70–73

accountability, 4–5, 12, 31–37; differentiated system for, 31, 34–36, 72; national database of schools in, 31, 37; for science and social science, need for, 37–43; state systems for, 21, 32–33; for subgroup problems, 34, 35–36

Achieve, Inc., 19, 22, 23

adaptive tests, 26, 30–31, 31n26

adequate yearly progress, 21, 26–31; in academic growth below proficiency threshold, 26–27; beyond proficiency, 28–29; growth models on, 27–29, 45; national database on, 31, 37; needs improvement. *See* needs-improvement schools; school accountability for, 31–37; and school choice options, 55–56, 57, 58, 59; subgroup problems in, 34, 35–36; and Supplementary Education Services, 60, 63, 66

African American students, academic achievement of, vii; as below basic level, 1, 2n1, 9; improvements in NAEP scores, 12; in private school choice, 54; as proficient or advanced, 9n6

Alabama, proficiency thresholds in, 20

American Diploma Project, 22

Annual Measurable Objectives, 71

AYP. *See* adequate yearly progress

Black students, academic achievement of, vii; as below grade level, 1, 2n1, 9; improvements in NAEP scores, 12; in private school choice, 54; as proficient or advanced, 9n6

"bubble kids," 33n31

Bush, George W., 4

California, proficiency scores in, 19

career readiness. *See* college and career readiness

28–30; financial rewards to schools in, 26, 29–30; lack of school incentives for, 27–28; state accountability systems in, 33

High Objective Uniform State Standard of Evaluation (HOUSSE), 50

high school education: exit requirements in, 23–24, 29; required for college or career, 19, 22, 23–24. *See also* college and career readiness

Hill, Paul, x

Hispanic students, academic achievement of: as below grade level, 1, 2n1, 9; improvements in NAEP scores, 12; as proficient or advanced, 9n6

history and social sciences, 9, 37–43; lack of progress in, 14–15; testing on, 41–42, 43; topics included in, 41

HOUSSE (High Objective Uniform State Standard of Evaluation), 50

Hoxby, Caroline, x

incentives: in accountability systems, 31, 32; for adaptive test development, 30–31; for schools with high-achieving students, 26, 29–30; for value-added teacher measurement and rewards, 52

Indiana, academic achievement standards in, 19

information systems: annual school report cards in, 37, 43; need for comprehensive education information system, 43–47; on school accountability status, 31, 37; on students eligible for Supplementary Education Services, 64–65

Japan, after-school tutoring in, 61

Koret Task Force on K-12 Education, ix, x

labor market, readiness for. *See* college and career readiness

Loveless, Tom, x

lowest achieving students, 13–14; state accountability systems in, 33

Massachusetts, proficiency thresholds in, 19, 20

mathematic skills, 7n4, 7–8; core standards on, 72; emphasis on, affecting science and social science teaching, 37–40, 43; importance of, 38; improvements in scores on, 12n14, 12–15, 14n16, 32; international assessment of, 7n4, 10

McKay scholarships, 55

Milwaukee, private school voucher programs in, 54

Mississippi, proficiency thresholds in, 20

Missouri, proficiency scores in, 19

Moe, Terry, x

NAEP. *See* National Assessment of Education Progress

national academic standards, 17, 22–26; based on efforts of three state consortia, 24, 25

National Assessment of Education Progress, 1n1, 2, 7n4, 7–14; below basic level of achievement in, 2n1, 8–9; core standards and tests compared to, 24–25; as high standard, 9, 9n9; improvements of scores in, 12n14, 12–15, 14n16, 32; international tests compared to, 9n9, 12n14; proficiency bar, 20; on science and social sciences, 42; and state accountability systems, 32; state test scores compared to, 20–21

National Council of Teachers of Mathematics, 7n4, 12n14

National Diploma Project, 25

EDUCATION
next
B O O K S

EDUCATION NEXT BOOKS address major subjects related to efforts to reform American public education. This imprint features assessments and monographs by Hoover Institution fellows (including members of the Hoover Institution's Task Force on K–12 Education), as well as those of outside experts.

Advancing Student Achievement
Herbert J. Walberg
(published by Education Next Books, 2009)

Learning from No Child Left Behind:
How and Why the Nation's Most
Important but Controversial Education
Law Should Be Renewed
John E. Chubb
(published by Education Next Books, 2009)

Reroute the Preschool Juggernaut
Chester E. Finn, Jr.
(published by Education Next Books, 2009)

Courting Failure:
How School Finance Lawsuits Exploit
Judges' Good Intentions and Harm Our
Children
Edited by Eric A. Hanushek
(published by Education Next Books, 2006)

Charter Schools against the Odds
Edited by Paul T. Hill
(published by Education Next Books, 2006)

Within Our Reach:
How America Can Educate Every Child
Edited by John E. Chubb
(published by Rowman & Littlefield, 2005)

Our Schools and Our Future
…Are We Still at Risk?
Edited by Paul E. Peterson
(published by Hoover Institution Press, 2003)

Choice with Equity
Edited by Paul T. Hill
(published by Hoover Institution Press, 2002)

School Accountability
Edited by Williamson M. Evers and
Herbert J. Walberg
(published by Hoover Institution Press, 2002)

A Primer on America's Schools
Edited by Terry M. Moe
(published by Hoover Institution Press, 2001)

OF RELATED INTEREST:
Education and Capitalism: How
Overcoming Our Fear of
Markets and Economics Can Improve
America's Schools
Edited by Herbert J. Walberg and
Joseph L. Bast
(published by Hoover Institution Press, 2003)